SENCHAKU HONGAN NEMBUTSU SHŪ

A COLLECTION OF PASSAGES ON THE
NEMBUTSU CHOSEN IN THE ORIGINAL VOW

BDK English Tripiṭaka 104-II

SENCHAKU HONGAN NEMBUTSU SHŪ

A Collection of Passages on the Nembutsu
Chosen in the Original Vow

Compiled by Genkū (Hōnen)

(Taishō Volume 83, Number 2608)

Translated into English

by

Morris J. Augustine

and

KONDŌ Tesshō

**Numata Center
for Buddhist Translation and Research
1997**

First Printing, 1997
ISBN: 1-886439-05-2
Library of Congress Catalog Card Number: 97-069168

Published by
Numata Center for Buddhist Translation and Research
2620 Warring Street
Berkeley, California 94704

Printed in the United States of America

A Message on the Publication of the English Tripiṭaka

The Buddhist canon is said to contain eighty-four thousand different teachings. I believe that this is because the Buddha's basic approach was to prescribe a different treatment for every spiritual ailment, much as a doctor prescribes a different medicine for every medical ailment. Thus his teachings were always appropriate for the particular suffering individual and for the time at which the teaching was given, and over the ages not one of his prescriptions has failed to relieve the suffering to which it was addressed.

Ever since the Buddha's Great Demise over twenty-five hundred years ago, his message of wisdom and compassion has spread throughout the world. Yet no one has ever attempted to translate the entire Buddhist canon into English throughout the history of Japan. It is my greatest wish to see this done and to make the translations available to the many English-speaking people who have never had the opportunity to learn about the Buddha's teachings.

Of course, it would be impossible to translate all of the Buddha's eighty-four thousand teachings in a few years. I have, therefore, had one hundred thirty-nine of the scriptural texts in the prodigious Taishō edition of the Chinese Buddhist canon selected for inclusion in the First Series of this translation project.

It is in the nature of this undertaking that the results are bound to be criticized. Nonetheless, I am convinced that unless someone takes it upon himself or herself to initiate this project, it will never be done. At the same time, I hope that an improved, revised edition will appear in the future.

It is most gratifying that, thanks to the efforts of more than a hundred Buddhist scholars from the East and the West, this monumental project has finally gotten off the ground. May the rays of the Wisdom of the Compassionate One reach each and every person in the world.

NUMATA Yehan
Founder of the English
Tripiṭaka Project

August 7, 1991

Editorial Foreword

In January, 1982, Dr. NUMATA Yehan, the founder of the Bukkyō Dendō Kyōkai (Society for the Promotion of Buddhism), decided to begin the monumental task of translating the complete Taishō edition of the Chinese Tripiṭaka (Buddhist Canon) into the English language. Under his leadership, a special preparatory committee was organized in April, 1982. By July of the same year, the Translation Committee of the English Tripiṭaka was officially convened.

The initial Committee consisted of the following members: HANAYAMA Shōyū (Chairperson); BANDŌ Shōjun; ISHIGAMI Zennō; KAMATA Shigeo; KANAOKA Shūyū; MAYEDA Sengaku; NARA Yasuaki; SAYEKI Shinkō; (late) SHIOIRI Ryōtatsu; TAMARU Noriyoshi; (late) TAMURA Kwansei; URYŪZU Ryūshin; and YUYAMA Akira. Assistant members of the Committee were as follows: KANAZAWA Atsushi; WATANABE Shōgo; Rolf Giebel of New Zealand; and Rudy Smet of Belgium.

After holding planning meetings on a monthly basis, the Committee selected 139 texts for the First Series of translations, an estimated one hundred printed volumes in all. The texts selected are not necessarily limited to those originally written in India but also include works written or composed in China and Japan. While the publication of the First Series proceeds, the texts for the Second Series will be selected from among the remaining works; this process will continue until all the texts, in Japanese as well as in Chinese, have been published.

Frankly speaking, it will take perhaps one hundred years or more to accomplish the English translation of the complete Chinese and Japanese texts, for they consist of thousands of works. Nevertheless, as Dr. NUMATA wished, it is the sincere hope of the Committee that this project will continue unto completion, even after all its present members have passed away.

It must be mentioned here that the final object of this project is not academic fulfillment but the transmission of the teaching of the

Buddha to the whole world in order to create harmony and peace among mankind. Therefore, any notes, such as footnotes and endnotes, which might be indispensable for academic purposes, are not given in the English translations, since they might make the general reader lose interest in the Buddhist scriptures. Instead, a glossary is added at the end of each work, in accordance with the translators' wish.

To my great regret, however, Dr. NUMATA passed away on May 5, 1994, at the age of 97, entrusting his son, Mr. NUMATA Toshihide, with the continuation and completion of the Translation Project. The Committee also lost its able and devoted Chairperson, Professor HANAYAMA Shōyū, on June 16, 1995, at the age of 63. After these severe blows, the Committee elected me, Vice-President of the Musashino Women's College, to be the Chair in October, 1995. The Committee has renewed its determination to carry out the noble intention of Dr. NUMATA, under the leadership of Mr. NUMATA Toshihide.

The present members of the Committee are MAYEDA Sengaku (Chairperson), BANDŌ Shōjun, ISHIGAMI Zennō, ICHISHIMA Shōshin, KAMATA Shigeo, KANAOKA Shūyū, NARA Yasuaki, SAYEKI Shinkō, TAMARU Noriyoshi, URYŪZU Ryūshin, and YUYAMA Akira. Assistant members are WATANABE Shōgo and MINOWA Kenryō.

The Numata Center for Buddhist Translation and Research was established in November, 1984, in Berkeley, California, U.S.A., to assist in the publication of the BDK English Tripiṭaka First Series. In December, 1991, the Publication Committee was organized at the Numata Center, with Professor Philip Yampolsky as the Chairperson. To our sorrow, Professor Yampolsky passed away in July, 1996, but thankfully Dr. Kenneth Inada is continuing the work as Chairperson. The Numata Center has thus far published eleven volumes and has been distributing them. All of the remaining texts will be published under the supervision of this Committee, in close cooperation with the Translation Committee in Tokyo.

MAYEDA Sengaku
Chairperson
Translation Committee of
the BDK English Tripiṭaka

June 1, 1997

Publisher's Foreword

The Publication Committee works in close cooperation with the Editorial Committee of the BDK English Tripiṭaka in Tokyo, Japan. Since December 1991, it has operated from the Numata Center for Buddhist Translation and Research in Berkeley, California. Its principal mission is to oversee and facilitate the publication in English of selected texts from the one hundred-volume Taishō Edition of the Chinese Tripiṭaka, along with a few major influential Japanese Buddhist texts not in the Tripiṭaka. The list of selected texts is conveniently appended at the end of each volume. In the text itself, the Taishō Edition page and column designations are provided in the margins.

The Committee is committed to the task of publishing clear, readable English texts. It honors the deep faith, spirit, and concern of the late Reverend Doctor NUMATA Yehan to disseminate Buddhist teachings throughout the world.

In July 1996, the Committee unfortunately lost its valued Chairperson, Dr. Philip Yampolsky, who was a stalwart leader, trusted friend, and esteemed colleague. We follow in his shadow. In February 1997, I was appointed to guide the Committee in his place.

The Committee is charged with the normal duties of a publishing firm—general editing, formatting, copyediting, proofreading, indexing, and checking linguistic fidelity. The Committee members are Diane Ames, Brian Galloway, Nobuo Haneda, Charles Niimi, Koh Nishiike, and the president and director of the Numata Center, Reverend Kiyoshi S. Yamashita.

Kenneth K. Inada
Chairperson,
Publication Committee

June 1, 1997

Contents

Contents

Translator's Introduction

Hōnen Shōnin's *A Collection of Passages on the Nembutsu Chosen in the Original Vow (Senchaku hongan nembutsu shū,* hereafter abbreviated as *Collection* and *Senchakushū*) is one of the most important Buddhist texts to be written in Japan during her long history. It ranks along with Dōgen Zenji's *The Treasured Eye of the True Dharma (Shōbōgenzō)* and with Hōnen's disciple Shinran's major writings as one of the three most influential bodies of Buddhist teachings of the Kamakura period. Together, the doctrinally revolutionary ideas contained in these works radically and permanently changed the face of Japanese Buddhism. And among them Hōnen's *Senchakushū* was, in terms of its originative and transformative effects on Japanese Buddhism, the most powerful of them all.

This very important work, unlike Dōgen's, is not at all difficult to understand. In fact its central message is so simple that any child could understand it. And therein precisely lies the secret of its unprecedented success. It brought Buddhism within the grasp of even the most unlettered peasant. In a word, Hōnen simply declares that Śākyamuni Buddha left an "easy way" for the powerless people of the Age of the Dharma's Degeneration into which the world has already entered. One need only cast aside all other worries and practices and recite the Nembutsu. All other Buddhist traditions, practices, and official sects—lumped together as the Gateway of the Holy Path— were expounded for stronger people of an earlier age. But now, says Hōnen, literally no one is able to use the Holy Path to attain Enlightenment. And so only the Gateway of the Pure Land—the simple recitation of the Nembutsu in full faith—can lead one to Rebirth in the Pure Land and assure one of eventual complete Enlightenment.

1

Though this central message is crystal clear in Hōnen's work, his sometimes tortured interpretations of scriptural passages, offered in an attempt to bring the various teachings of the three Chinese patriarchs into some semblance of logical coherence, are not. Only careful scholarly research into the slow development of Chinese and Japanese Pure Land tradition can unravel the complexities involved.

Three things should be kept in mind while reading this central work of Hōnen: (1) Hōnen's own central role in founding the new Pure Land Sect (Jōdo Shū) and, via his disciple Shinran, of originating the True Pure Land Sect (Jōdo Shin Shū) as well (these two new sects eventually came to include the vast majority of all Buddhist believers and practitioners in Japan), (2) the origins and nature of the doctrines that are set forth in the *Collection*, and (3) the precise difference between Hōnen's teachings as set forth in this document and the even more revolutionary teachings and writings of his disciple Shinran.

Regarding the first of these points, it is important to understand from the beginning that Hōnen did not himself originate more than a small portion of the ideas contained in this his major work, the *Collection*. He himself is the best witness that the three Chinese patriarchs of the Pure Land tradition, T'an-luan, Tao-ch'o, and Shan-tao, were the source for the great majority of the passages in his *Collection*, especially Shan-tao (613–681), who was dead more than five hundred years before Hōnen (1133–1212) was born, and on whom Hōnen relied for practically the whole of the teachings presented in the *Collection*.

Hōnen was nevertheless a truly great originator in that it was he (his disciple Shinran began by merely following in his master's footsteps) who almost singlehandedly created the revolutionary movement that was eventually to transform the very nature of most of Japanese Buddhism. Relying on Shan-tao, whose works he had come to rely on only after many years of less radical Pure Land practice, Hōnen taught that one must completely abandon the practice of every other Buddhist observance or discipline and rely solely on the verbal and continual recitation of the phrase "Namu Amida Butsu" or "Homage to Amida Buddha" with firm faith. By this "easy way" one can be reborn into Amida's Pure Land in the West at death and there be absolutely assured of eventual complete Enlightenment. Hōnen, however, pushed these teachings of Shan-tao a step further. He argued that his teaching or school (*shū*) was in fact one of the legitimate, independent, fully recognized sects (the same word, *shū*, but with a vastly augmented significance) of Buddhism. And in fact this *Collection* (*Senchakushū*) was a major force in the eventually successful fight for precisely such public and official recognition.

However, once having given Hōnen his rightful place among the patriarchs of Japanese Buddhism, we must immediately qualify his revolutionary status by situating him in the middle of a long Pure Land tradition in Japan, one that began almost with the original introduction of Buddhism into Japan in the fourth and fifth centuries. But Pure Land belief and Nembutsu practice were, until Hōnen's revolution, usually understood to be a relatively minor part of the elaborate scheme of doctrines, practices, and meditative disciplines of one of the six officially recognized sects of Japanese Buddhism. Each of the traditional recognized sects, such as the Tendai, the Shingon, and the older Nara sects, had its own unique combination of such absolutely required elements, and the recitation of the Nembutsu—though encouraged as one "easy" way—was never considered to be even a central element of any of them. Even Genshin (942–1017), the author of the immensely influential *A Collection on the Essentials for Rebirth in the Pure Land* (*Ōjōyōshū*), with all of its inspiring images of the glories of Amida's Pure Land, never dreamed of demanding, as Hōnen was to do roughly two hundred years later, that the practitioner completely abandon every other Buddhist practice and rely on the Nembutsu alone.

Regarding the second of the above three central points, the origins of the teachings and practices that Hōnen sets down in his *Collection*, it must suffice here to enlarge only slightly upon what was said above, that Hōnen relied almost exclusively on Shan-tao's writings to ground his own teachings. This is clearly evident in the present work, especially in the overwhelming priority of place given to quotations from Shan-tao's writings in Hōnen's *Collection*. The precise meaning and nature of Hōnen's major work and its title can be clearly understood only in this light. It is, as the title implies, nothing more than a collection of recognized scriptural authorities marshalled and interpreted with the intent of proving the orthodoxy of a radical Pure Land exclusivism, a teaching and practice that, even while Hōnen was still alive, was immediately and bitterly condemned by the entrenched traditional sects. The central contention of Hōnen's *Collection* is that Amida "chose" (the "*Senchaku*" of the title) only the Nembutsu and set it up as the one practice carefully tailored to save not only the weakest of men and women, but the strongest as well, in this degenerate age.

The source of Hōnen's teachings can be traced more precisely, first to the Threefold Sutra of the Pure Land (see the Glossary), second to the general Pure Land tradition, which from very early times runs throughout the major schools of the Mahayana tradition, third to a Pure Land tradition and practice deeply entrenched before Hōnen, and finally and more precisely to the above-mentioned three Pure Land patriarchs, especially Shan-tao. A more precise overview of the nature of each of these sources of Hōnen's work and teachings can be gleaned by carefully consulting the alphabetized Glossary at the end of this work, which explains every scriptural reference, every technical doctrinal term or phrase, and every person mentioned by Hōnen in his *Collection*.

The third difficult point that needs brief explanation here is the somewhat disputed matter of precisely how Hōnen's teaching as presented in the present work differs from that of his famous disciple Shinran. The first thing to note here is Shinran's own protestation that every word of his own teaching derived from that of his beloved master Hōnen. Proof of his sincerity in this regard lies in the fact that he copied the whole of the present work in his own hand. The fact is, however, that Shinran brought Hōnen's rendering of Shan-tao's ideas — actually Shinran relied more on Tao-ch'o — to an even more radical stage.

Shinran declares that the practitioner in our Age of Degeneration cannot even wish to recite the Nembutsu, much less perform more difficult works, without the enabling omnipresent power of Amida's Original Vow to save all sentient beings. Hōnen, however, insists throughout the present work that men and women can and must recite the Nembutsu as the one and only "practice" left within their power. Whereas he does see this recitation as based on Amida's Other Power, he nevertheless uses the same terminology (e.g., "practice") and the same manner of thinking as that used by others within his mother Tendai sect. In other words, people retain some small power of their own to do good, and thus an absolutely total break with traditional Buddhism was avoided. Such is the essence of the difference between the teaching of Hōnen and that of his disciple, though volumes have been written about the nuances of the controversy.

The present translation of Hōnen's *A Collection of Passages on the Nembutsu Chosen in the Original Vow* is the result of some fifteen years of collaborative labor between its two translators. I wish to acknowledge my esteemed collaborator as being also my teacher in the realm of her Master, Hōnen. During the endless long hours, weeks, months, and years in which we collaborated, I learned not only the teachings of Hōnen but—at least imperfectly—the inner difficult discipline of Kanbun (Japanese writing in the Chinese language) and to understand and deeply respect the inner heart and mind of a kind of Buddhist thought and practice that I had never before seriously confronted. All of this has been immensely enriching. Finally, as a comparative historian of religions I have come to appreciate the important place that the "new" Pure Land schools of Hōnen and Shinran occupy in the ranks of the world's great and influential religious systems.

Morris J. Augustine

Chapter I

The Two Gateways

Namu Amida Butsu
The Nembutsu is foremost among the
practices for Rebirth in the Pure Land

*Passages Concerning How Tao-ch'o, the Dhyāna Master,
Distinguishing between Two Gateways—the Holy Path and the
Pure Land—Cast Aside the Holy Path and Sincerely Took
Refuge in the Pure Land*

In the first volume of the *Collection of Passages on the Land of*   1b
Peace and Bliss [by Tao-ch'o] we read:

> One might ask, "If all sentient beings have the Buddha na-
> ture, and as each of them from ancient times to the present
> must have encountered many Buddhas, why then do they
> still continue through cycles of birth and death and fail to
> escape from this burning house?" To such a question, I
> should answer that according to the holy teaching of the
> Mahayana, it is actually because they have been unable to
> cast aside birth and death through exercising one of the
> two kinds of the excellent Dharma, that they have not been
> able to escape from the burning house.

7

What then are these two kinds? One is called the Holy Path and the other is called Rebirth in the Pure Land. In these days it is difficult to attain Enlightenment through the Holy Path. One reason for this is that the Great Enlightened One's passing has now receded far into the distant past. Another is that the ultimate principle is profound, while human understanding is shallow. That is why it is stated in the *Candragarbha Sūtra* that "In the Period of the Dharma's Decadence, after I [Śākyamuni] will have passed away, even though countless sentient beings should begin to practice and cultivate the Way, not a single one of them will attain the goal." Now we are in the Age of the Dharma's Decadence, that is, the evil world of the Five Defilements. The Gateway of the Pure Land is the only one through which we can pass to Enlightenment. Thus it is stated in the *Larger Sutra* that "If there should be a single sentient being who, even having committed evil deeds throughout life, recites my Name ten times without interruption as death draws near, and yet fails to be reborn in my Pure Land, then may I never attain Enlightenment."

Further, no one among all sentient beings is able to weigh his own spiritual abilities. From the Mahayana point of view, no one has yet contemplated Suchness, the true reality, or Emptiness, the most fundamental principle. From the Hinayana point of view, one must enter into the Path of Insight and the Path of Practice, then one must work one's way up through the Stage of the *Anāgāmin* to that of the Arhat, severing the Five Bonds of the Lower World of Desires and leaving behind the Five Bonds of the Higher Worlds of Form and Formlessness. Until now, however, neither monk nor layperson has ever been able to reach these goals. True, there are those who enjoy the benefit of being born as human or heavenly beings. But this benefit is achieved only by having practiced the Five Precepts and the Ten Virtues. Now, however, even those who continue to observe these precepts and virtues are very rare.

When, on the other hand we consider people's evil doings and sinful deeds, are they not raging everywhere like storm winds and lashing rains? It is because of these things that the many Buddhas, in their immense compassion, urge us to take refuge in the Pure Land. For even though someone has done evil all his life, if only he is able to practice the Nembutsu continually, attentively, and single-mindedly, then all obstacles will spontaneously disappear and he will certainly attain Rebirth in the Pure Land. Why, indeed, do men fail to take heed of these things? And why are they not determined to forsake this world for the Pure Land?

My own opinion, after quietly pondering these matters, is that the manner of officially presenting the Buddha's teachings differs somewhat among the various schools. To begin with the Idealist school, we see that it divides the lifetime teachings of the Buddha into the Three Periods: (1) the period when he affirmed the reality of phenomenal things, (2) the period when he declared phenomenal things to be "empty" of reality, and (3) the period when he taught the Middle Way, which transcends these two opposites.

The Emptiness school divides the lifetime teachings of the Buddha into two canons: one for the Bodhisattva and one for the *Śrāvaka*.   1c

The Hua-yen school formulated the Five Teachings embracing the whole of the Buddha's message: the Hinayana, the Beginning, the Final, the Sudden, and the Perfect Teaching. The Lotus [or T'ien-t'ai] school formulated the Four Teachings and the Five Flavors, embracing the whole of the Buddhist teaching. The Four Teachings are those of the Hinayana Canon and the Common, Particular, and Perfect Teachings. The Five Flavors are those of milk, cream, butter, cheese and ghee. The Shingon [or Mantra] school formulated the Two Teachings, which encompass the whole of Buddhism. They are the Exoteric and Esoteric Teachings.

Regarding the Pure Land school now under discussion, we see that it has—if we rely on the Dhyāna Master Tao-ch'o—set up the Two Gateways encompassing the whole of the Buddha's message: the Gateway of the Holy Path and the Gateway of the Pure Land.

Someone might ask, "The names of the eight or nine schools—Kegon (Hua-yen), Tendai (T'ien-t'ai) and so on—have long been officially recognized, but I have never heard the group of Pure Land devotees officially designated as a 'school.' Therefore what proof can you offer to justify your references to the 'Pure Land school'?"

In answer to such a query, I would say that there is more than one testimony justifying the appellation "Pure Land school." In Yüan-hsiao's *The Light Heart in the Way of Peace and Bliss* it is stated that, "The Pure Land school was originally meant to save ordinary men and, at the same time, it is also for Holy Men." Furthermore, in Tz'u-en's *The Essentials for Rebirth in the Western Paradise* it is stated, "We rely on this school alone." And yet again in Chia-ts'ai's *Treatise on the Pure Land* it is stated that, "This particular school is, I believe, the essential Way." Such being the testimonies, there should be no room for doubt.

My present concern, however, is not to discuss the foundations of the various schools. Rather, turning to the Pure Land school, I shall briefly clarify the matter of the Two Gateways. One of these is the Gateway of the Holy Path and the other is the Gateway of the Pure Land.

First, the Gateway of the Holy Path is divided into two parts: one is the Mahayana and the other is the Hinayana. The Mahayana is further divided into the Exoteric and Esoteric, as well as the Provisional and the Real. In the *Collection of Passages on the Land of Peace and Bliss* only the Exoteric and the Provisional Teachings of the Mahayana are treated. Hence, the Holy Path Teachings refer to the circuitous or "gradual" forms of practice, which require many kalpas. From this we can infer that the Holy Path Teachings also include the Esoteric and the Real. It follows then that the teachings of all eight contemporary schools—the Shingon, Busshin, Tendai, Kegon, Sanron, Hossō, Jiron, and Shōron—are also included in the Holy Path. We ought to be aware of this.

Next, the Hinayana is the Way for the *Śrāvaka* and the *Pratyekabuddha* as explained in the Hinayana sutras, monastic rules (*vinaya*), and *śāstra*s. It is the way of realizing the truth by cutting off deluding passions, thereby attaining the ranks of Holy

Men and realizing spiritual fruition. Hence, we can infer here as before that the Holy Path also includes the Realist, the *Satyasiddhi,* and the various Vinaya schools.

Generally speaking, then, the main purport of the Gateway of the Holy Path, whether Mahayana or Hinayana, concerns practicing the Way of the Four Vehicles and attaining the fruit of the Four Vehicles while in this Saha world. In speaking of the Four Vehicles, we are referring to the Three Vehicles with the addition of the Buddha Vehicle. 2a

Turning next to the Gateway of Rebirth in the Pure Land, we find that here too there are two teachings. First, there are those that directly expound Rebirth in the Pure Land. Second, there are those teachings that only incidentally expound this Rebirth.

The first one—"those teachings that directly expound Rebirth in the Pure Land"—is set forth in the so-called "three sutras and one *śāstra.*" The first of these is the *Sutra of Immeasurable Life,* the second is the *Meditation Sutra,* and the third is the *Amida Sutra.* The "one *śāstra*" is the *Treatise on Rebirth in the Pure Land* by Vasubandhu. The "three sutras" are also called the "Threefold Sutra of the Pure Land."

Someone may ask whether or not there are any other instances where the phrase "Threefold Sutra" can be found. The answer is that it has appeared more than once. One such instance is the Threefold Lotus Sutra in which the three sutras are the *Sutra of Infinite Meaning,* the *Lotus Sutra,* and the *Samantabhadra Meditation Sutra.* A second instance is the Threefold Mahāvairocana Sutra, namely, the *Mahāvairocana Sutra,* the *Diamond Crown Sutra,* and the *Sutra of Excellent Accomplishment.* A third example is the Threefold Sutra for the Peace and Protection of the State: the *Lotus Sutra,* the *Benevolent King Sutra,* and the *Golden Light Sutra.* A fourth is the Threefold Sutra of Maitreya: the *Sutra of Maitreya's Ascending Birth,* the *Sutra of Maitreya's Descending Birth,* and the *Sutra on Maitreya's Becoming a Buddha.* Here we are concerned only with the Threefold Sutra about Amida, which I call the Threefold Sutra of the Pure Land. It is the scripture upon which the Pure Land teaching is properly based.

Next, "teachings that only incidentally expound Rebirth in the Pure Land" are the sutras that expound Rebirth in the Pure Land, such as the *Garland Sutra*, the *Lotus Sutra*, the *Wish-fulfilling Dhāraṇī Sutra*, the *Dhāraṇī Sutra on the Most August One*, and others. They also include treatises such as the *Awakening of Faith*, the *Treatise on the Precious Nature*, the *Treatise Explaining the Ten Stages*, the *Compendium of the Mahayana*, and similar works that expound Rebirth in the Pure Land.

Now the reason why Tao-ch'o, in his *Collection*, set up the distinction between the Two Gateways of the Holy Path and the Pure Land was to teach people to reject the Gateway of the Holy Path in favor of entering the Gateway of the Pure Land. There are two reasons for this preference: one is that the passing away of the Great Enlightened One has now receded far into the distant past, and the other is that the ultimate principle is profound while man's understanding is shallow.

Tao-ch'o is not the only one in the Pure Land school who set up this distinction of the Two Gateways. T'an-luan, T'ien-t'ai, Chia-ts'ai, Tz'u-en, and many other teachers all have the same view.

To begin with Dharma Master T'an-luan, we see that he stated in his *Commentary on the Treatise on Rebirth in the Pure Land*:

> Let us reverently reflect on what the Bodhisattva Nāgārjuna said in his *Treatise Explaining the Ten Stages*. He declared that there are two paths by which the Bodhisattvas may seek the Stage of Non-Retrogression: one is the Way of Difficult Practice and the other is the Way of Easy Practice. The Way of Difficult Practice is a way of trying to reach the Stage of Non-Retrogression in an Age of the Five Defilements when no Buddha dwells in the world. This is difficult to do. This difficulty takes many forms and I should like to mention a few of them to exemplify what I mean.
>
> First there is the merely apparent good of non-Buddhist teachers who bring confusion into the true Dharma of the Bodhisattva. Second there is the self-interest involved in the *Śrāvaka*'s discipline, which interferes with great compassion.

Third, there is the evil done without reflection, which destroys the excellent virtues of others. Fourth, there is the result of good deeds based on deluded thinking, which corrupts pure and undefiled practice. Fifth, there is the holding on to self power alone and not taking hold of Other Power. These are things everywhere to be seen. To follow this Way of Difficult Practice is like travelling overland on foot: it is very painful and hard. 2b

The Way of Easy Practice is to desire Rebirth in the Pure Land only by means of faith in the Buddha. Being thus carried along by the power of the Buddha's Vows, we shall be able to attain Rebirth in the Pure Land. The Buddha's power will sustain us and enable us to enter into the company of those who have attained the Stage of Genuine Assurance of the Mahayana. This is the Stage of Non-Retrogression. It is like taking passage on a ship and sailing over the sea: it is very pleasant.

In this context, the Way of Difficult Practice is the Gateway of the Holy Path, and the Way of Easy Practice is the Gateway of the Pure Land. Difficult Practice as distinct from Easy Practice and Holy Path as distinct from Pure Land; the words differ but the meaning is actually the same. The Masters T'ien-t'ai and Chia-ts'ai share the same view. We surely ought to be aware of this.

Again, as is stated in *The Essentials for Rebirth in the Western Paradise*:

As I reverently reflect on the matter, it is clear that Śākyamuni appeared at an opportune time and benefitted all those who were karmically related to him. He extended his teaching to accommodate people's different natures and thus watered all the people with the dew of the Dharma. Those who met the Holy Teacher personally were each led toward Enlightenment along one of the Ways of the Three Vehicles. He encouraged those whose goodness was slight and who were negligent in proper karmic practice to take refuge in the Pure Land. Anyone who engages in this practice will be reborn in that Land by meditating exclusively on Amida and turning over the merits of all his good deeds toward Rebirth. Amida, in his Original Vow, resolved to ferry beings from this Saha world to the other shore. All those engaging in this practice—who at best continue it for the whole of their lives, but who at least think of Amida ten times when they are on the verge of death—will certainly attain Rebirth.

Again, in the postscript to the same work it is said:

If we carefully reflect, we will realize that we have been born near the end of the Age of the Semblance of the Dharma, long after the Holy One's passing. Although we are acquainted with the Way of the Three Vehicles, we cannot attain Enlightenment through it. Both men and *deva*s are filled with the agitation and unrest of the deluding passions. Those whose wisdom is great and whose hearts are opened wide in compassion may be able to abide long in samsara, practicing the Way. But the foolish and those whose practice lacks depth will probably sink into the dark realms of inferior states of being. We should by all means, therefore, remove ourselves far from this Saha world and let our hearts dwell in the Pure Realm.

In this passage, the "Three Vehicles" refers to the Gateway of the Holy Path, and the "Pure Realm," the Gateway of the Pure Land. As for "Three Vehicles" as distinct from "Pure Realm" and "Holy Path" as distinct from "Pure Land"—these phrases differ in name but their meaning is actually the same.

He who would learn of the Pure Land school should first of all understand the import of the above passages. Even though a man may have previously studied the Gateway of the Holy Path, if he feels an inclination toward the Gateway of the Pure Land, he should set aside the Holy Path and take refuge in the Pure Land. An example of one who did this was the Dharma Master T'an-luan, who abandoned his lecturing on the Four Treatises and wholeheartedly sought the shelter of the Pure Land. The Dhyāna Master Tao-ch'o abandoned his manifold activities in studying and teaching the *Nirvana Sutra* and began to propagate the practice of the Pure Land of the West exclusively. Such was the case with the wise and learned masters of old. Why, then, should we foolish men in the Age of the Dharma's Decadence fail to follow their example?

Someone may raise the following question. The various schools and sects of the Holy Path each have their own direct line of master–disciple transmission of the Dharma. In the case of the T'ien-t'ai school, for example, the genealogy is from Hui-wen to Nan-yüeh, to T'ien-t'ai, to Chang-an, to Chih-wei, to Hui-wei, to Hsüan-lang, to Chan-jan. In the case of the Shingon school, the successive transmission is from Mahāvairocana Tathāgata to Vajrasattva, to Nāgārjuna, to Nāgabodhi, to Vajrabodhi, to Amoghavajra. Likewise, each of the many remaining schools has its own "artery" through which its transmission flows. Is there any such artery of successive teachers in the Pure Land school?

I would reply to such a question by pointing out that the Pure Land school does indeed have its own arteries of transmission just like those of the Holy Path. However, in this particular school of the Pure Land there are several differing "houses." These are the houses of the Dharma Master Hui-yüan of Lu-shan, of the Tripiṭaka Master Tz'u-min, and of Tao-ch'o and Shan-tao. Here we will limit ourselves to the lineage advocated by Tao-ch'o and Shan-tao and discuss its artery of Dharma transmission. Concerning it, there are two opinions. According to one—found in the *Collection of Passages on the Land of Peace and Bliss*—the succession is as follows: the Tripiṭaka Master Bodhiruci, the Dharma Master Hui-ch'ung, the Dharma Master Tao-ch'ang, the Dharma Master T'an-luan, the Dhyāna Master Ta-hai, and the Dharma Master Fa-shang. According to the other—found in the biographies of eminent masters of both the T'ang and Sung Dynasties—the succession began with the Tripiṭaka Master Bodhiruci, who was followed by the Dharma Master T'an-luan, the Dhyāna Master Tao-ch'o, the Dhyāna Master Shan-tao, the Dharma Master Huai-kan, and the Dharma Master Shao-k'ang.

Chapter II

The Right and Miscellaneous Practices

Passages That Relate How Master Shan-tao Distinguished between the Two, "Right" and "Miscellaneous," Kinds of Practice, Rejecting the Miscellaneous and Taking Refuge in the Right

Shan-tao says in the fourth book of his *Commentary on the Meditation Sutra*:

> As to establishing faith in practice, we should first note that practice is of two kinds: Right and Miscellaneous. The Right consists in performing only the kinds of discipline derived from the sutras on Rebirth in the Pure Land, hence the name "Right Practices." What disciplines are they? They are:
>
> (1) Single-mindedly and wholeheartedly chanting the *Meditation Sutra*, the *Amida Sutra,* and the *Sutra of Immeasurable Life*;
>
> (2) Single-mindedly and wholeheartedly thinking on, contemplating, and remembering the adornments of the two recompenses in that Land;
>
> (3) When doing reverence is in order, single-mindedly and wholeheartedly doing reverence to that Buddha;
>
> (4) When uttering [holy names] is in order, single-mindedly and wholeheartedly uttering the Name of that Buddha;
>
> (5) When giving praises and offerings is in order, single-mindedly and wholeheartedly giving them [to Amida].

These are called the Right [Practices]. Further, within these Right Practices there are two types. The first is to concentrate single-mindedly and wholeheartedly on the Name of Amida, whether walking or standing still, whether seated or lying down, without considering whether the time involved is long or short and without ceasing even for an instant. This is called the Right Established Act. It is so called because such a practice agrees with the intent of Amida's Vow. Other practices, such as doing reverence to the Buddha and chanting [sutras], are called the Auxiliary Acts. Besides these two—the Right Established and the Auxiliary Practices—all the other good practices are collectively called Miscellaneous Practices.

If we perform the Right and the Auxiliary Practices, our heart always remains intimate with and near [to Amida], and we never cease to remember him. Hence these are called the Incessant. However, when we perform the other Miscellaneous Practices, our concentration is always liable to be broken. Even though we can indeed be reborn by transferring the merit [of such practices to that end], they are called Estranged Miscellaneous Practices.

In my own view this passage has two purposes. The first is to make clear the types of practice proper for Rebirth. The second is to determine the advantages and disadvantages of the two kinds of practice.

3a

1. Types of Practice Proper for Rebirth

As to the first, elucidation of the practices proper for Rebirth, according to Master Shan-tao, the practices leading to Rebirth are many but can be grouped under two major divisions: the Right and the Miscellaneous Practices.

Speaking first of the Right Practices, there are two [ways of elucidating their] import: the "divided" and the "merged." In the first, they are divided into five kinds; later they are merged into two.

First, regarding the division into five kinds:

(1) The Right Practice of Sutra-Chanting
(2) The Right Practice of Contemplation
(3) The Right Practice of Doing Reverence
(4) The Right Practice of Uttering the Name
(5) The Right Practice of Giving Praises and Offerings

The first, the Right Practice of Sutra-Chanting, is to chant the *Meditation Sutra* and the other [Pure Land] sutras wholeheartedly; or in the words of the above-quoted passage, "single-mindedly and wholeheartedly chanting the *Meditation Sutra*, the *Amida Sutra,* and the *Sutra of Immeasurable Life*." The second, the Right Practice of Contemplation, is to contemplate the two recompenses—principal and dependent—of that Land wholeheartedly; or as we read in the text above, "single-mindedly and wholeheartedly thinking on, contemplating, and remembering the adornments of the two recompenses." The third, the Right Practice of Doing Reverence, is to do reverence wholeheartedly to Amida Buddha, or as in the text above, "when doing reverence is in order, single-mindedly and wholeheartedly doing reverence to that Buddha." The fourth, the Right Practice of Uttering the Name, is to utter the Name of Amida Buddha wholeheartedly, or as in the words of the text above, "when uttering [holy names] is in order, single-mindedly and wholeheartedly uttering the Name of that Buddha." The fifth, the Right Practice of Giving Praises and Offerings, is to give praises and offerings wholeheartedly to Amida; or as in the text above, "when giving praises and offerings is in order, single-mindedly and wholeheartedly giving them [to Amida]. These are called the Right (Practices)." If we treat "praising" and "making offerings" as two separate acts, then we must speak of "the six kinds of Right Practice." Here these two are joined together and so we speak of "the five kinds of practice."

Next, regarding the two "merged" practices: the Right Act and the Auxiliary Acts. First, the Right Act is uttering the Name, which is the fourth of the above-listed five kinds of Right Practice, namely the Right Established Act. It is as is stated in the above passage:

To concentrate single-mindedly and wholeheartedly on the Name of Amida, whether walking or standing still, whether seated or lying down, without considering whether the time involved is long or short and without ceasing even for an instant. This is called the Right Established Act. It is so called because such a practice agrees with the intent of Amida's Vow.

Next, the Auxiliary Acts are the four other kinds of acts, such as sutra-chanting, with the exception of the fourth, uttering (the Name). This is as is stated in the above passage:

Other practices, such as doing reverence to the Buddha and chanting [sutras], are called the Auxiliary Acts.

It may be asked, "Why, among the five kinds of practice, is only uttering the Name of Amida Buddha called the Right Established Act?" I answer that it is because this is in accord with the intent of Amida's Vow. That is to say, uttering the Name of Amida is the practice referred to in the Original Vow of the Buddha. Therefore, the one who is dedicated to this practice is carried forward by the power of Amida's Vow and will certainly attain Rebirth in the Pure Land. The meaning of the Buddha's Original Vow will be made clear below.

We shall next discuss the Miscellaneous Practices. Above, we read the following words:

Besides these two—the Right Established and the Auxiliary Practices—all the other good practices are collectively called Miscellaneous Practices.

The meaning is this: there being endless numbers of such Miscellaneous Practices, we do not have the time here to discuss them in detail. We now only briefly explain the five kinds of Miscellaneous Practice corresponding to the five kinds of Right Practice:

(1) The Miscellaneous Practice of Sutra-Chanting
(2) The Miscellaneous Practice of Contemplation
(3) The Miscellaneous Practice of Doing Reverence
(4) The Miscellaneous Practice of Uttering [Holy Names]

(5) The Miscellaneous Practice of Giving Praises and
        Offerings

Regarding the first, the Miscellaneous Practice of Sutra-Chanting, with the exception of the above-mentioned *Meditation Sutra* and others pertaining to Rebirth in the Pure Land, cherishing and chanting the sutras, whether Mahayana or Hinayana, whether Exoteric or Esoteric, is called the Miscellaneous Practice of Sutra-Chanting.

Regarding the second, the Miscellaneous Practice of Contemplation, with the exception of the above-mentioned contemplation of the principal and dependent recompenses in the Land of Supreme Bliss, all practices of contemplation, whether of phenomenal things or of underlying principles, whether pertaining to Mahayana or Hinayana, Exoteric or Esoteric, are called the Miscellaneous Practices of Contemplation.

Regarding the third, the Miscellaneous Practice of Doing Reverence, with the exception of the above-mentioned reverence to Amida, all forms of worshipping and showing reverence to Buddhas and Bodhisattvas, as well as to the various divinities, are called the Miscellaneous Practice of Doing Reverence.

Regarding the fourth, the Miscellaneous Practice of Uttering [Holy Names], with the exception of the above-mentioned practice of uttering the Name of Amida, all forms of the practice of uttering the names of Buddhas and Bodhisattvas, as well as the names of various divinities, are called the Miscellaneous Practice of Uttering [Holy Names].

Regarding the fifth, the Miscellaneous Practice of Giving Praises and Offerings [to Holy Beings], with the exception of the above-mentioned practice of giving praises and offerings to Amida Buddha, all forms of giving praises and offerings to Buddhas and Bodhisattvas, as well as to various divinities, are called the Miscellaneous Practice of Giving Praises and Offerings [to Holy Beings].

In addition to these five, there are also countless numbers of other practices, such as charity and observance of the precepts. All of these should be included under the name of Miscellaneous Practice.

2. The Advantages and Disadvantages of the
Two Kinds of Practice

Next, I will judge the advantages and disadvantages of the two kinds of practice. It is said in the above quotation:

> If we perform the Right and the Auxiliary Practices, our heart always remains intimate with and near [to Amida], and we never cease to remember him. Hence these are called Incessant. However, when we perform the other Miscellaneous Practices, our concentration is always liable to be broken. Even though we can indeed be reborn by transferring the merit [of such practices to that end], they are called Estranged Miscellaneous Practices.

Considering the merits of these words, we find that with regard to these two—the Right and the Miscellaneous Practices—there are five pairs of contrasts:

> (1) The Intimate versus the Estranged
> (2) The near versus the far
> (3) The Intermittent versus the Incessant
> (4) Transference of merit versus no transference of merit
> (5) The Pure versus the Miscellaneous

As regards the first pair, the Intimate versus the Estranged, "Intimate" means that those who perform both the Right and the Auxiliary Practices are brought into exceedingly close intimacy with Amida Buddha. Thus we read in the preceding part [i.e., the third book] of the *Commentary*:

> When sentient beings arouse themselves to practice and always utter with their lips the Name of the Buddha, the Buddha will hear them. When they constantly and reverently bow down to the Buddha, the Buddha will see them. When they continually think of the Buddha in their hearts, the Buddha will know them. When sentient beings remember the Buddha, the Buddha also remembers them. In these

3c

22

three acts, the Buddha and sentient beings are not separate from each other. Hence, they are called the intimate relation.

Next, "Estranged" refers to Miscellaneous Practices. When sentient beings do not call the Buddha, the Buddha does not hear them. When they do not bow down to the Buddha, the Buddha does not see them. When they do not think of the Buddha in their hearts, the Buddha does not know them. When they do not remember the Buddha, the Buddha does not remember them. In these three acts, the Buddha and the sentient beings are separate from each other. Hence, they are called "Estranged Practices."

As regards the second pair, the near versus the far, "near" means that those who perform the two—the Right and the Auxiliary—Practices are very near to Amida Buddha. Thus in the preceding part of the *Commentary* we read:

> If sentient beings desire to see the Buddha, he, responding to this desire, will appear before their eyes. Hence, this is called the near relation.

Next, "far" refers to the Miscellaneous Practices. If sentient beings do not desire to see the Buddha, he will respond to this lack of desire and not appear before their eyes. Hence, they are called "far."

The meanings of "intimate" and "near" seem to be identical but Shan-tao distinguishes between them. This appears in his *Commentary*. Therefore, I have quoted these passages here and explained them.

As regards the third pair, the Incessant versus the Intermittent, "Incessant" means that those who perform the two—the Right and Auxiliary—Practices never cease to remember Amida Buddha. Hence, this is called "Incessant."

Next, "Intermittent" means that those who perform Miscellaneous Practices will constantly find their concentration on Amida Buddha broken. That is why it is said, "our concentration is always liable to be broken."

As regards the fourth pair, "no transference of merit" versus "transference of merit," those who perform the two—the Right and the Auxiliary—Practices, even though they do not deliberately intend to transfer the merit [of these practices toward attaining Rebirth], will nevertheless see that their practice by its very nature becomes a Rebirth practice. Thus we read in the preceding part of the *Commentary*:

> Now the 'ten utterances of the Buddha's Name' in this *Meditation Sutra* contain and accomplish the Ten Vows and the Ten Practices. How do they accomplish them? 'Namu' means 'to take refuge.' It also means 'to desire to transfer one's merits.' 'Amida Butsu' is the practice. For this reason, one can surely attain Rebirth [by reciting it].

Next, "transference of merit" means that those who perform the Miscellaneous Practices can make them serve as sufficient cause for Rebirth only when they intend their merits to be transferred [to this end]. When they do not intend merit-transference, then their practice does not become sufficient cause for Rebirth. That is why it is said, "Even though we can indeed be reborn by transferring the merit [of such practices to that end] . . ."

As regards the fifth pair, the Pure versus the Miscellaneous, "Pure" refers to the performance of the two—the Right Established and the Auxiliary—Practices, which are the Pure Practices leading to Rebirth in the Land of Supreme Bliss. Next, the Miscellaneous Practices are not practices leading directly to the Land of Supreme Bliss. They are common to those beings who [seek rebirth as] human and heavenly beings, who [follow] the Three Vehicles or who [seek rebirth in other] Pure Lands of the ten directions. Therefore they are called "Miscellaneous." Hence practitioners longing for the Western Land should necessarily cast aside the Miscellaneous and perform the Right Practice.

It may be asked whether evidence for this understanding of the Pure and the Miscellaneous Practices can be found in the sutras and treatises. The answer is that there is more than one instance in the sutras, Vinayas, and treatises of both Mahayana and Hinayana in which the Two Gateways of Pure and Miscellaneous Practices

4a

are distinguished. The Mahayana establishes the "miscellaneous storehouse" among the eight storehouses. It should be understood that seven of these eight are pure, and one miscellaneous. The Hinayana sets up the *Miscellaneous Āgama* as one of the four *Āgama*s. It should be understood that three of them are pure and one is miscellaneous. In the [*Four-Part*] *Vinaya*, twenty sections are established to explain practice in accord with the precepts. Among these, the first nineteen are pure and the last one is miscellaneous. In an [*Abhidharma*] treatise, eight sections are distinguished to explain the nature and aspects of various dharmas. The first seven are pure and the last is miscellaneous. In the various collections of wise and holy men's biographies from the T'ang and Sung dynasties, we read that the virtuous conduct of the noble monks is explained under the ten headings. Of these, the first nine are pure and the last is miscellaneous. Furthermore, in *A Collection of Passages on the Profound Meaning of the Mahayana* there are five groups of Dharma gateways, of which the first four are pure and the last is miscellaneous. Further, not only in the Exoteric Teachings but also in the Esoteric Teachings there are pure and miscellaneous Dharmas. It is stated in the *Records of the Lines of the Dharma Transmission* [by the Master Saicho] of the Tendai school:

> The first is the record of the Matrix Realm Mandala line of transmission.
> The second is the record of the Diamond Realm Mandala line of transmission.
> The third is the record of the Miscellaneous Mandala line of transmission.

The first two are pure and the last is miscellaneous. The cases in which the pure-versus-miscellaneous mode of classification is employed are many. Here I have briefly presented only a few of them. It should be noted that, in their various contexts, the significations of pure and miscellaneous are not fixed. In the light of this, the intention of the Master Shan-tao in the above passage was to discuss the pure and miscellaneous with regard to Pure Land practice. The notion of the pure versus miscellaneous is not limited to canonical Buddhist writings. Very many examples are also found in non-Buddhist sources. In order to avoid unnecessary tedium, I shall not treat these here.

Shan-tao is not the only master who divides practices for Rebirth in the Pure Land into two kinds. According to the view of the Dhyāna Master Tao-ch'o, practices for Rebirth [in the Pure Land] are many but are grouped in two categories: (1) Rebirth through the Nembutsu and (2) Rebirth through the myriad practices. Next, according to the view of the Dhyāna Master Huai-kan, practices for Rebirth in the Pure Land are also many but are grouped in two categories: (1) Rebirth through the Nembutsu and (2) Rebirth through the various practices. (Eishin makes the same division.) These three masters have indeed made a very appropriate interpretation when each sets up two kinds of practice to group practices for Rebirth. Other masters did not make such a division. Practitioners should certainly take note of this fact.

It is stated in the *Hymns in Praise of Rebirth*:

> If people practice the Nembutsu continuously in the above-mentioned manner until the end of their lives, then ten out of ten practitioners will attain Rebirth, and a hundred out of a hundred will attain Rebirth. Why is this so? It is because this practice keeps away other miscellaneous karmic conditions and enables one to achieve right mindfulness. It is because it accords with the intent of the Buddha's Original Vow. It is also because it does not contradict the teaching. Further, it is because it is in accord with the Buddha's words.
>
> As for those who choose to cast aside the whole-hearted practice and perform Miscellaneous Practices, it is rare for even one or two out of a hundred, or even four or five out of a thousand, to attain Rebirth. Why? It is because their practice is disturbed by miscellaneous karmic conditions and so they lose Right Mindfulness. It is because their practices do not accord with the Buddha's Original Vow. It is because

4b

they differ from the Teaching. It is because they are not in accord with the Buddha's words. It is because these people do not keep their minds continually fixed [on Amida Buddha]. It is because their concentration is broken. It is because they do not really have a sincere desire to transfer their merits toward Rebirth. It is because the passions of greed, anger, and wrong views arise and disrupt [their concentration on Amida]. It is because they lack repentance and contrite hearts. Moreover, it is because they do not remember this Buddha continually to repay their indebtedness to him. It is because pride arises in their hearts and, though they engage in practice, they always have a desire for fame and self-benefit. It is because their hearts are filled with attachment to their fellow practitioners and teachers. It is because they seek miscellaneous karmic conditions and so they create hindrances for themselves and others in the performance of the Right Practices for Rebirth.

Why do I make these assertions? It is because I have myself recently seen and heard that everywhere practitioners, whether monks or laity, differ from one another in understanding and practice and in particular with regard to the wholehearted and Miscellaneous Practices. Only people who concentrate their minds on their practice will attain Rebirth, ten people out of ten. As for people who perform Miscellaneous Practices and so fail to attain sincerity of heart, not even one out of a thousand will be reborn. The advantages and disadvantages of these two practices have already been stated above.

It is my desire that those wishing to be reborn should carefully weigh their own capacities. Those who already in this lifetime desire Rebirth in the Land should unfailingly exert themselves in the performance of this practice, whether moving or standing still, whether sitting or lying down; they should conquer their own egos and should never cease practicing, day and night, until the end of their lives.

To practice this way all through life may appear to be somewhat painful, but when life comes to an end, the very next moment they will be reborn into that Land, where they will continue to enjoy the bliss of unconditioned [nirvana] throughout the length of eternal kalpas. Until they attain Buddhahood, they will never again have to pass through the cycles of birth and death. Is this not a joyful thing? One should take careful note of it.

I believe that anyone who reads these words ought to cast aside the Miscellaneous and take up the Exclusive Practice. Why should anyone cast aside the Exclusive and Right Practice, by which a hundred out of a hundred attain Rebirth, and stubbornly cling to the Miscellaneous Practices, by which not even one out of a thousand attains Rebirth? Practitioners ought seriously to ponder this.

Chapter III

The Original Vow

*The Passage Concerning Amida Tathāgata's Original Vow,
Which Promised Rebirth Not for Other Practices but for the
Nembutsu Only*

It is said in the first volume of the *Sutra of Immeasurable Life*:

> If, upon my attainment of Buddhahood, all sentient beings
> in the ten directions who, aspiring in all sincerity and faith
> to be born in my Land, utter my Name [lit. "Think (of me)"]
> even ten times are not reborn there, then may I not attain
> Supreme Enlightenment.

This passage as it appears in the *Dharma Gate of Contemplation*
reads as follows:

> If, when I become a Buddha, all sentient beings in all the
> ten directions, who desire to be born in my Land and utter
> my Name at least ten times, are not reborn there through
> the power of my Vow, then may I not attain Supreme En-
> lightenment.

4c

The same passage is again quoted in the *Hymns in Praise of Rebirth* as follows:

> If, when I become a Buddha, all sentient beings in all the
> ten directions who utter my Name at least ten times are not
> reborn, then may I not attain Supreme Enlightenment. That
> Buddha is at present in his Land, having already attained
> Buddhahood. Therefore we should surely realize that the
> weighty promise of the Original Vow was not made in vain:
> If sentient beings recite the Nembutsu, they will certainly
> attain Rebirth.

My explanation is that each one of all the Buddhas made two kinds
of Vows: general and special. The general ones are known as the
four universal vows. The special ones are those such as the five
hundred great vows of Śākyamuni and the twelve superior vows
of the Tathāgata Bhaiṣajyaguru. The Forty-eight Vows now under consideration are the special Vows of Amida.

It may be asked, "When and under what Buddha's guidance
did the Tathāgata Amida make these Vows?" In answer I would
quote the *Sutra of Immeasurable Life*:

> The Buddha said to Ānanda, "In the distant past, very long,
> immeasurable, unthinkable, and uncountable kalpas ago,
> the Tathāgata Dīpaṅkara came into the world and taught
> and emancipated countless sentient beings, enabling them
> all to achieve the Buddha Way. Then he entered nirvana.
> Next there came into the world a Tathāgata named Prata-
> pavat, and so on, and the next Tathāgata was called Lokendra.
>
> "These Buddhas, fifty-three in all, having passed away,
> another Buddha by the name of Lokeśvararāja came into
> the world. At that time, there lived a king. When he heard
> the Buddha's explanation of the Dharma, his heart was filled
> with joy, and an aspiration for the Unsurpassable Supreme
> Enlightenment was awakened in his mind. Leaving his
> country and abandoning the throne, he took up the ascetic
> practice of a Śramaṇa and called himself Dharmākara. He
> surpassed all others in ability and intelligence and went to
> the Tathāgata Lokeśvararāja . . .

"Then the Buddha Lokeśvararāja described to him in detail the good and the evil aspects of human and heavenly beings in the Lands of twenty-one billion Buddhas and also the coarse and refined aspects of those Lands. Then in accordance with Dharmākara's request, he actually showed them all to him. Having heard the discourse of the Buddha on the magnificent Pure Lands and having seen them all, the Bhikṣu Dharmākara made his unsurpassable and truly admirable Vows. His heart being quiet and tranquil and his will unattached, no one in all the world could equal him. For five kalpas he pondered the pure practices needed in order to establish a superior Buddha Land, and he made them his own."

Ānanda then asked the Buddha, "How long was the Buddha's life span in that [Lokeśvararāja's] Land?" The Buddha answered, "That Buddha's life span was forty-two kalpas. Eventually, the Bhikṣu Dharmākara succeeded in making his own the pure practices through which the twenty-one billion Buddhas established their refined Lands."

In the *Larger Amida Sutra* we read:

The Buddha then chose from among the good and evil human and heavenly beings living in the twenty-one billion Buddha Lands, and also chose from among the pleasant and unpleasant features of those Lands. Then he chose the Vows [that accorded with] the desires of his heart. 5a

When Lokeśvararāja Buddha (also referred to here as Sovereign King of the World) finished his exposition, Dharmākara (also referred to here as Dharma Storehouse) concentrated his mind so intensely that he attained the vision of divine beings. With this penetrating sight he himself saw all the good and the evil aspects of human and heavenly beings and also the pleasant and the unpleasant features of the twenty-one billion Buddha Lands. Then he himself chose the Vows [which accorded with] the desires of his own heart. It is thus that he made the Twenty-four

Vows. (The same account is also found in the *Sutra of Universal Enlightenment.*)

"Chose" in the above passage means "take up some thing while rejecting other things." This means that he [Dharmākara] rejected the evil aspects of the human and heavenly beings in the twenty-one billion Buddha Lands and took up their good aspects; he rejected the unpleasant features of these Lands and took up the pleasant ones. This is the meaning of "choose" in the *Larger Amida Sutra*. In the context of the *Two-Volume Sutra* [i.e. the *Sutra of Immeasurable Life*] there is also the notion of "choose"; that is to say, it is found in the passage above, ". . .succeeded in making his own the pure practices through which the twenty-one billion Buddhas established their refined Lands." "Choose" and "make his own" are two different forms but their meaning is the same. It follows then that he rejected the impure practices and took up the pure ones. With reference to the above-mentioned choosing from among the good and the evil aspects of human and heavenly beings and among the coarse and the refined features of the Lands, the same interpretation applies. We should know this from the above explanation.

Now, the meaning of "to choose" and "to make one's own" will be briefly discussed in relation to each of the Forty-eight Vows. The first Vow was that none of the Three Evil Realms should be present. Among the twenty-one billion Buddha Lands [which Dharmākara saw] there were some where these Three Evil Realms existed and some where they did not. Dharmākara chose to reject the coarse and inferior Lands where the Three Evil Realms existed and chose to make his own the good and refined Lands where they did not. Hence the word "choose."

The second Vow was that no one would return to the Evil Realms. Even though in some of the many Buddha Lands the Three Evil Realms do not exist, still the human and heavenly beings there, after their lives are over, leave those Lands and return to the Three Evil Realms. On the other hand, there are other Lands from which there is no returning to the Evil Realms. Dharmākara chose to reject the coarse and inferior Lands from which we would return to the Evil Realms and chose to make his own the good and refined Lands from which there is no returning to the Evil Realms. Hence the word "choose."

The third Vow was that everyone should be of golden color. In the Buddha Lands there are some wherein both yellow and white human and divine beings live together. There are also Buddha Lands wherein all beings are of a pure golden color. Thus, Dharmākara chose to reject the coarse and inferior Lands in which there existed yellow and white beings, and he chose to make his own the good and refined Lands where the color of all beings is pure gold. Hence the word "choose." 5b

The fourth Vow was that there should be no differentiation between beauty and ugliness. Among the many Buddha Lands there are some wherein human and divine beings are unequal with respect to beauty or ugliness of face and form. There are other Buddha Lands whose inhabitants have one and the same physical appearance and there is no distinction with respect to their beauty or ugliness. Thus Dharmākara chose to reject the coarse and inferior lands where beauty and ugliness are unequal and chose to make his own the good and refined lands where such inequality does not exist. Hence the word "choose."

[Proceeding in the same manner] one comes to the Eighteenth Vow concerning Rebirth through the Nembutsu. Among these many Buddha Lands there are some wherein Rebirth is attained through the practices of almsgiving. Again, there are some wherein Rebirth comes through observance of the precepts. In other Lands, the practice for Rebirth is patience; in others it is zeal, and in others it is meditation. Again, in other lands, the Rebirth practices is *Prajñā*—that is, knowledge of the supreme reality. There are also lands wherein Rebirth comes through the Bodhi mind, in others through the six acts of mindfulness, in others by chanting sutras, and again in others by *dhāraṇī* recitation. Further, there are lands wherein Rebirth is attained by performing various practices such as erecting stupas and making images of the Buddha, offering food to Śramaṇas, being dutiful to parents, and venerating teachers and elders. Also there are lands wherein Rebirth is obtained by the wholehearted recitation of the names of the Buddhas of those Lands.

To conclude that a certain practice is thus allotted for Rebirth in the land of a certain Buddha is a superficial interpretation. However, if we reconsider the matter, it is clear that it is not the definitive one. In certain Buddha Lands Rebirth is obtained by many practices, while in many others it is obtained by a single practice common to all. In this way, we find that the practices for Rebirth are of many different kinds. It is not possible to discuss them all in detail.

Here [in the Eighteenth Vow], he [Dharmākara] chose to cast aside various practices, such as the above-mentioned almsgiving, observance of the precepts, and lastly filial piety, and chose to make his own the wholehearted recitation of the Buddha's Name. Hence the word "choose."

I have above briefly discussed the notion of "to choose" in five of the Vows. Its meaning is as shown above. The meaning of "to choose" in the remaining Vows can accurately be deduced from this.

It may be asked, "It seems reasonable that he [Dharmākara] should in this way have chosen to cast aside the coarse and inferior and take up the good and refined elements in all his Vows; but why did he, in the Eighteenth Vow, choose to cast aside all other practices and take up the Nembutsu alone? Why did he make his Original Vow of Rebirth [only to those who practice it]?"

I would answer by saying that although the Buddha's Holy Intention is difficult to fathom and impossible to understand fully, 5c   it may best be interpreted with the aid of the following two notions: (1) superior versus inferior and (2) difficult versus easy.

Firstly, as regards superior versus inferior, the Nembutsu is superior and the other practices are inferior. This is because the Name is the container into which all of [Amida's] uncountable virtues have flowed. That is to say, in the Name are contained all the merits and virtues of Amida's inner Enlightenment, such as the four wisdoms, the three bodies, the ten powers, and the four fearlessnesses. Also contained in it are all the merits and virtues from which his outward activities flow, such as the major and minor bodily characteristics, the emanations of light, the preaching of the Dharma, and the granting of benefits to sentient beings. For these reasons, the merits and virtues of the Name are incomparably "superior." The other practices are not the same as this; each one of them is only good for producing a limited portion of merit and virtue. For this reason, they are called "inferior."

Let me offer the metaphor of an ordinary house to explain this. The name "house" includes all of its constituent elements: the ridgepole, the rafters, the beams, the pillars, and so on, but none of the names—"ridgepole," "rafter," and so on—can denote the entire "house." From this we see that the merits and virtues of the Buddha's Name are superior to those of all other practices. It is in this sense that Dharmākara cast aside the inferior and took up the superior when he made his Original Vow.

Secondly, as regards difficult versus easy, the Nembutsu is easy to practice while the other practices are difficult to perform. That is why it is said in the *Hymns in Praise of Rebirth*:

> It may be asked, "Why are we not urged to practice meditation but urged in a straightforward manner to utter wholeheartedly the Name?" In answer, I say that this is because the karmic bonds of sentient beings are heavy, the objects of meditation subtle, their minds desultory, their attention wavering, and their spirits jumping about, and so it is difficult for them to succeed in meditation. For this reason, the Great Holy One, moved with pity, straightforwardly encouraged them to utter the Name wholeheartedly. Since uttering the Name is really easy, we are able to continue this practice and attain Rebirth.

And again, in the *Collection on the Essentials for Rebirth* we read:

> It may be asked, "All good practices are meritorious, and each can lead to Rebirth. Why is it that the Gateway of the Nembutsu alone is encouraged?" In answer, I would say that

when I now urge everyone to practice the Nembutsu, I do
not intend to set aside the various other superior practices.
What I mean to say is that the Nembutsu is not difficult to
perform for either man or woman, whether highborn or low,
whether walking, standing still, sitting, or lying down, and
no matter when, where, and under what karmic conditions.
And finally, when anyone is on his deathbed and desires to
be reborn, no practice is more accessible than the Nembutsu.

It is, therefore, clear that since the Nembutsu is easy, it is open to
everyone, while the various other practices are not open to all types
of people, because they are difficult. Was it not in order to bring all
sentient beings without exception to Rebirth that [Dharmākara]
in his Original Vow cast aside the difficult practices and chose the
easy one?

If the Original Vow had required us to make images of the
Buddha and to build stupas, the poor and the destitute would certainly have to give up hope of Rebirth, but the fact is that the rich
and the highborn are few, while the poor and the lowborn are
exceedingly many. If the Original Vow required us to have wisdom and intelligence, the foolish and the unwise would certainly
have to give up hope for Rebirth, but the fact is that the wise are
few, and the foolish are very numerous. Again, if the Original Vow
6a required us to hear and read many things, those who have heard
and read little would certainly have to give up hope of Rebirth,
but the fact is that those who have heard much are few and those
who have heard little are very many. Further, if the Original Vow
required us to observe the precepts and abide by the rules for
monks' behavior, those who have broken the precepts and those
who have never undertaken them would certainly have to give up
hope of Rebirth, but the fact is that those who observe the precepts are few, while those who have broken the precepts are exceedingly many. As for the various other practices, they should be
understood in the same way.

We should know that if the Original Vow required us to perform the manifold practices above, then those who are able to attain

Rebirth would be few and those unable to do so would be very many. For this reason, Amida Tathāgata, in the distant past when he was the Bhikṣu Dharmākara, moved with an impartial compassion and wishing to save all beings universally, did not choose in his Original Vow concerning Rebirth the manifold practices, such as making images of the Buddha and building stupas. He chose the single practice of uttering the Nembutsu in that Original Vow.

Thus, the Dhyāna Master Fa-chao writes in his *Five Tone Ceremonial Hymns* [*Aspiring for Rebirth in the Pure Land*]:

> That Buddha made a Universal Vow when he was in the
> causal stage [of Bodhisattvahood]:
> "I shall come to welcome all those who hear my Name and
> meditate on me.
> No distinction will be made between the poor and rich,
> between the destitute and the noble;
> No distinction between those of slight wisdom and those
> of great talent;
> No preference given to those who have heard much and
> who observe the precepts
> Over those who have broken the precepts and those who
> have deep-rooted karmic sins.
> If only they turn their hearts to me and recite many
> Nembutsus,
> Like broken tiles and pebbles turned into gold, [they will
> attain salvation].

It may be asked, "All the Bodhisattvas have made vows. Some have already fulfilled their vows, while others have not yet done so. I wonder whether or not Dharmākara's Forty-eight Vows have already been fulfilled." I would answer that each of his Vows has been fulfilled. The reason I say so is that already in the World of Supreme Bliss there are none of the Three Evil Realms; we should know that the Vow that there be none of the Three Evil Realms has already been fulfilled. How can we know this? It is said in the passage regarding the fulfillment of the Vow: "Hell, the realms of hungry ghosts and animals, and the various afflictions do not exist." This is how we know.

Further, humans and *deva*s of that country, after the end of their lives, do not return to the Three Evil Realms. We should know then that the Vow that there would be no returning to the Evil Realms has been fulfilled. How can we know this? It is said in the passage regarding the fulfillment of the Vow: "Further, the Bodhisattvas of that Land will never return to the Evil Realms even up to the time when they become Buddhas." This is how we know.

Further, there is no human or *deva* in the World of Supreme Bliss who does not possess the thirty-two physical characteristics [of a Bodhisattva]. We should know that the Vow that everyone would possess the thirty-two physical characteristics has been fulfilled. How do we know this? In the passage regarding the fulfillment of the Vow we read "Those who are born in that Land possess the thirty-two physical characteristics." This is how we know.

In the same way, from the first Vow that there should exist none of the Three Evil Realms to the last Vow that one should attain the three Dharma insights, each and every one of the Vows has been fulfilled. Then is there any reason why the Eighteenth Vow concerning Rebirth through the Nembutsu should be the only one not to be fulfilled? It follows then that all who practice the Nembutsu will be reborn.

6b

In the passage regarding the fulfillment of the Vow of Rebirth through the Nembutsu we read:

> If sentient beings hear his Name and, rejoicing with believing hearts, think of him even once while single-heartedly transferring their merits in the desire for Rebirth in his Land, then they will attain Rebirth and abide in the State of Non-Retrogression.

In general, it is the Forty-eight Vows that have embellished the Pure Land. The lotus ponds and jewelled palaces would not exist except for the power of the Vows. Why, then, among all those Vows, should the Vow of Rebirth through the Nembutsu be the only one that we should doubt? Moreover, it is said at the end of each Vow, "If not, may I not attain Supreme Enlightenment." We must note here that ten kalpas have already elapsed since Amida attained Buddhahood and so the Vow to become a Buddha has already been fulfilled. Therefore, we should surely know that none of these Vows was made in vain. This is why Shan-tao says:

> The Buddha has attained Buddhahood and is at present dwelling in his World. We should surely know that the weighty promise of the Original Vow was not made in vain. If sentient beings recite the Nembutsu, they will surely be reborn.

It may be asked, "In the sutra it says 'think of [me] ten times,' while in [Shan-tao's] interpretations it says 'utter ten times.' How should we understand the meaning of 'think of' and 'utter'?" I should say in answer that "think of" and "utter" are really one thing. How do we know this? The *Meditation Sutra*, in expounding to the lowest level of the lowest class of beings, says:

> If we utter "Namu Amida Butsu" with uninterrupted voice while thinking [of him as few as] ten times, then, because we utter the Buddha's Name, with each repetition our sins accumulated during the births and deaths of eight billion kalpas are removed.

Now, according to this passage, it is clear that "utter" means "think of" and "think of" is the same as "utter." Moreover, it is said in the *Candragarbha Sutra*, "With a great thought [of the Buddha] one sees a great Buddha; with a small thought one sees a small Buddha." Master Huai-kan's interpretation of this is, "'a great thought' means uttering the Nembutsu in a loud voice, and 'a small thought' means uttering the Nembutsu in a soft voice." Thus we know that "think of" is the same as "utter."

It may be asked, *"The [Larger] Sutra says 'even [ten times]'* while [Shan-tao's] interpretation says 'at least [ten utterances].' How do you explain this difference?" I would reply that "even" and "at least" have the same meaning. The word "even" in the sutra is a term which indicates "from many to few." "Many" indicates the upper limit of spending our whole life [in the practice of the Nembutsu]. "Few" indicates the lower limit of ten utterances or even one utterance. In the phrase "at least" in [Shan-tao's] interpretation, "least" is a term which contrasts with "most." "At least" means "down to ten utterances, or even one." "Most" means "going to the upper limit, covering one's whole life." There are many examples of passages contrasting "most" and "least." In the Vow to enable us to acquire the supernatural power of knowing our own and others' previous lives it is said:

> If, when I have become a Buddha, the men and *deva*s of my Land do not know their own or others' previous lives and the events of at least a hundred thousand *koṭi*s of *nayuta*s of kalpas in the past, then may I not attain Supreme Enlightenment.

Similarly, the term "at least" is used in each of the other Vows relating to the Five Supernatural Powers and the Vows of Light and Life. In all these cases, it means going from "many" to "few," and "least" stands in opposition to "most." Considering the usage of "at least" as it appears in the above eight Vows, we see that it has the same meaning as "even" in this [Eighteenth] Vow. Therefore, the phrase "at least" which is used here in Shan-tao's interpretation does not differ from that.

6c

Shan-tao's interpretation, however, is not the same as that of other masters. According to these other masters' interpretations, this Vow is taken in a limited sense and called "the Vow of Rebirth through uttering ten Nembutsus." Shan-tao alone interpreted it in a comprehensive sense and called it "the Vow of Rebirth through the Nembutsu." The other masters restricted the meaning of the Vow by calling it "the Vow of Rebirth through uttering ten Nembutsus." Their interpretation is not all-inclusive, for it excludes both the notion of upper limit of the lifelong Nembutsu practice, and that of its lower limit, a single utterance. When Shan-tao interpreted it in a comprehensive sense and called it "the Vow of Rebirth through the Nembutsu," his interpretation was all-inclusive, for it included both its upper and lower limits: the lifelong and the single Nembutsu.

Chapter IV

The Three Classes of People

*Passages Relating How All Three Classes of People Can Be
Reborn through the Nembutsu*

It is said in the second volume of the *Sutra of Immeasurable Life*:

> The Buddha said to Ānanda, "Generally speaking there
> are—among the many *deva*s and human beings in all the
> worlds of the ten directions—three classes of people who
> sincerely desire to be reborn in that Land. The man of the
> superior class leaves his home, renounces his desires, and
> becomes a Śramaṇa: he awakens in himself the Bodhi mind,
> single-mindedly and wholeheartedly meditates on the Bud-
> dha of Immeasurable Life, and desires to be reborn in that
> Land by devoting himself to the many meritorious prac-
> tices. When such a sentient being reaches the end of his
> life, the Buddha of Immeasurable Life, together with a great
> multitude [of Holy Beings], will appear before him. In the
> company of that Buddha, he will be reborn in Amida's Pure
> Land and take up his abode in the center of a seven-jewel-
> led flower; he will spontaneously attain Rebirth by a sud-
> den transformation and will abide in the Stage of
> Non-Retrogression. He will be endowed with wisdom, he-
> roic courage, and unrestricted supernatural powers.

"For this reason, Ānanda, those sentient beings who desire to see the Buddha of Immeasurable Life even while yet in this present life should without hesitation awaken in themselves the unsurpassed Bodhi mind, devote themselves to meritorious practices, and desire to be reborn in that Land."

The Buddha said to Ānanda, "The middle class is composed of those many *devas* and men in all the worlds of the ten directions who with sincere heart desire to be reborn in that Land. Even though they are unable to perform the practices of a Śramaṇa and thus amass a great store of merit, nevertheless they should awaken in themselves the unsurpassed Bodhi mind and meditate single-mindedly and wholeheartedly on the Buddha of Immeasurable Life; they should engage, to some degree at least, in the practice of good deeds, keep the precepts, make Buddha images, and build stupas; they should offer food to the Śramaṇas, adorn the Buddha's shrines with banners, light lamps, scatter flowers, and burn incense. They should turn the merits of these good deeds over toward Rebirth, with the desire to be reborn in that Land. When such people are on their deathbeds, the Buddha of Immeasurable Life will reveal himself to them in his transformed body. He will be emanating rays of light and will possess all of the major and minor physical characteristics of Buddhahood, being in every detail exactly like the true Buddha. He will reveal himself before these men together with a great multitude [of Holy Beings]. Then in the company of that Transformation Buddha, they will be reborn in that Land and abide in the Stage of Non-retrogression. In virtue and wisdom, they will rank next to the superior class."

7a   The Buddha said to Ānanda, "The lower class is composed of those many *devas* and men in all the worlds of the ten directions who sincerely desire to be reborn in that Land. Even though they are unable to perform manifold meritorious practices, they should awaken in themselves the unsurpassed

Bodhi mind, single-mindedly and wholeheartedly meditate even ten times on the Buddha of Immeasurable Life, and thus they should desire Rebirth in that Land. If they hear the profound Dharma with joy and faith, without entertaining any doubt, and meditate even once on that Buddha, desiring with sincere minds to be reborn in that Land, then at the end of their lives they will see that Buddha as if in a dream and be able to attain Rebirth. In virtue and wisdom, they will rank next to the middle class."

It may be asked, "In the passage regarding the superior class there are in addition to the Nembutsu, leaving one's home, renunciation of one's desires, and other practices. And in the passage concerning the middle class, there are also such practices as building stupas, making Buddha images, and the like. In the passage about the lower class too, there are other practices such as awakening in oneself the Bodhi mind and the like. Why are these called simply [practices for] Rebirth through the Nembutsu?"

I should answer with the words of Master Shan-tao from his *Dharma Gate of Contemplation*:

Furthermore, in the first part of the second volume of the *Sutra of Immeasurable Life* it is said: "The Buddha explained that the natures of all sentient beings are not equal. There are among them the superior, middle, and lower classes. The Buddha urged that everyone, each in accord with his own nature and character, should wholeheartedly dwell on the Name of the Buddha of Immeasurable Life. For those who do this, when they come face to face with their end, the Buddha himself, together with throngs of Holy Beings, will come to welcome them and enable each and every one of them to attain Rebirth."

According to this exposition, all three classes are said to attain Rebirth through the Nembutsu.

It may be objected that this explanation does not entirely answer the question, "Why do you abandon the other practices and speak only of the Nembutsu?" My answer is that this has three implications: (1) the manifold practices were expounded [only] so that one would be led to abandon them and take refuge in the Nembutsu, (2) the manifold practices were expounded to assist the Nembutsu, and (3) the manifold practices were expounded in order to set up the three classes of people within both of the Two Gateways: that of the Nembutsu and that of the manifold practices.

As to the first of these implications—that the manifold practices were expounded [only] so that one would be led to abandon them and take refuge in the Nembutsu—we read in Shan-tao's *Commentary on the Meditation Sutra*:

> Even though above we have expounded on the benefits of both gateways,—the gateways of the Contemplative and of Distractive Practices, nevertheless, [Śākyamuni's ultimate] intent—in the light of that Buddha's [Amida's] Original Vow—was to cause all sentient beings to utter single-mindedly and wholeheartedly the Name of Amida Buddha.

Briefly, the meaning of these words is as follows. Even though in the passage on the superior class, the awakening of the Bodhi mind and the various other practices were expounded, still, in the light of the Original Vow propounded previously, those practices were expounded only in order eventually to bring all sentient beings to do nothing other than to utter the Name of Amida Buddha. But in the Original Vow there are no other practices at all. Hence it is because all of the three classes depend on the Original Vow propounded previously that it is said, "[The man of the superior class] single-mindedly and wholeheartedly meditates on the Buddha of Immeasurable Life." "Single-mindedly" (*lit.* "in one direction") is a term that contrasts with "in two or more directions." To illustrate, in the five parts of India there are three kinds of temples. The first kind is devoted "single-mindedly" to the Mahayana. In these temples, no study is made of the Hinayana. The second kind is devoted "single-mindedly" to the Hinayana. In these temples, no study is made of the Mahayana. The third kind is devoted to both Mahayana and Hinayana practices. In these temples, Mahayana and Hinayana are studied together. Hence, they are called temples of "combined practice." Naturally, one understands that as regards both the Mahayana and the Hinayana temples, the term "single-mindedly" is used, whereas temples of "combined practice" do not use the term "single-mindedly." Exactly the same thing is true of the use of "single-mindedly" in the *Sutra [of Immeasurable Life]*. If one adds other practices to the Nembutsu, then the practice is not single-minded. In terms of the temple analogy, this would be called "combined practice."

Thus it becomes clear that what above was called "single-minded" is not combined with other things. In the passage above, the other practices are first expounded and afterward the "single-minded and wholehearted" Nembutsu is mentioned. Hence we clearly know that the term "single-minded" is employed to make people abandon the manifold practices and practice only the Nembutsu. If such were not the case, then would not the term "single-minded" be very difficult to interpret?

Turning to the second implication, there are also two meanings in the words, "The manifold practices were expounded to assist the Nembutsu." The first is that the Nembutsu is assisted by good practices that are [basically] the same kind [as the Nembutsu itself]. The second is that the Nembutsu is assisted by good practices of a different kind.

The first—that the Nembutsu is assisted by good practices of the same kind—is found in Master Shan-tao's *Commentary on the Meditation Sutra*. There he mentions five kinds of Auxiliary Practices that assist the single practice of the Nembutsu. This was explained in detail above in the chapter on "The Right and Miscellaneous Practices."

As regards the second—that the Nembutsu is assisted by good practices of a different kind—let us speak first of the Right and Auxiliary Practices that are performed by the superior class. "To meditate single-mindedly and wholeheartedly on the Buddha of Immeasurable Life" refers to the Right Practice. It is that which is assisted [by the others]. Whereas, "[The man of the superior class] leaves his home, renounces his desires, becomes a Śramaṇa, and awakens in himself the Bodhi mind," and so on, refers to the Auxiliary Practices. They are also those which assist [the Nembutsu]. That is to say, among the acts that lead to Rebirth, the Nembutsu is the basic act. Therefore it is in order to practice the Nembutsu single-mindedly that "the man of the superior class leaves his home, renounces his desires, becomes a Śramaṇa, and awakens in himself the Bodhi mind," and so on. The above-mentioned leaving home and awakening of the Bodhi mind here refer to leaving home for the first time and the first awakening [of the Bodhi mind]. However, the Nembutsu is a lifelong practice from which one never retreats. Why then should these other practices interfere with it?

In the middle class are found the manifold practices of building stupas and making Buddha images, decorating Buddha shrines with banners, lighting [votive] lamps, scattering flowers, burning incense, and so forth. These assist the Nembutsu. A reference to this interpretation is found in the *Collection on the Essentials for Rebirth*, where it says that "among the means for assisting the Nembutsu are selecting a suitable place, making proper offerings and decorations, and so on."

In the lower class, both the awakening of the Bodhi mind and the Nembutsu are found. The meanings of "Auxiliary" and "Right" are to be understood here in the same way as in the cases above.

The third implication is that the manifold practices were expounded in order to set up the three classes of people within both the Nembutsu practice and the manifold other practices.

First we shall discuss the establishment of the three classes of people within the Nembutsu practice. The passages referring to each of the three classes all mention "meditate single-mindedly and wholeheartedly on the Buddha of Immeasurable Life." This indicates that three classes of people were established for the Nembutsu Gateway. Thus the *Collection on the Essentials for Rebirth* says in the chapter "Testimony in Favor of the Nembutsu":

7c

> Even though shallow and deep practices are distinguished among the practices of three classes described in the *Sutra of Two Volumes*, they all include "single-mindedly and whole-heartedly thinking on the Buddha of Immeasurable Life."

(The same interpretation is made by Master Huai-kan.)

Next, "setting up three classes of people within the manifold practices" means that some of the practices—awakening the Bodhi mind and others—are also found in all three classes. In this way, the three classes of people were also set up in relation to the manifold practices as well. That is why it is stated in the chapter titled "The Gateway of Rebirth through the Manifold Practices" in the *Collection on the Essentials for Rebirth*, "[The practice for] the three classes described in the *Sutra of Two Volumes* do not go beyond this (i.e., practices for the nine levels of people)."

Generally speaking, even though the three implications discussed here are different, taken together, they all recommend the single-minded practice of the Nembutsu. Thus, according to the first implication, the manifold practices were taught for the sake of "abandonment and establishment." That is to say, the manifold practices were expounded in order that they might be abandoned; the Nembutsu was expounded in order that it might be established. The next implication is that the manifold practices were expounded for the sake of the Auxiliary and the Right. That is to say, the Auxiliary Acts that make up the manifold practices were taught so that they might assist the Right Practice, which is the Nembutsu. The final implication is that the manifold practices were taught in order to distinguish the "peripheral" and the "proper" practices. That is, even though the Two Gateways of the Nembutsu and the manifold practices were both taught by the Buddha, the Nembutsu was meant to be the proper one while the manifold practices were made to be the peripheral. That is why it is said that the Nembutsu is present in all of the practices [proper to each] of the three classes of people.

Regarding these three implications, it is difficult to distinguish which is inferior and which is superior. Therefore, I ask scholars to use their own discretion in deciding. However, if we rely on Shan-tao, we will take the first interpretation as the correct one.

One might ask, "The reason why the Nembutsu is among the practices for all three classes may be just as you say; it may further be noted that the difference between the nine levels of people in the *Meditation Sutra* and the three classes of the *Sutra of Immeasurable Life* is basically one of a 'combined' versus an 'expanded' mode of classification; but if that is so, why is it that for all three classes of people in the *Sutra of Immeasurable Life* mention is made of the Nembutsu, while in the section on the nine levels of the *Meditation Sutra*, the Nembutsu is not advocated for those beings in the superior and middle levels but only for those of the lower level?"

I would say in answer that there are two possible interpretations. The first is what was stated in the above question: namely, "The difference between the three classes of the *Sutra of Two Volumes* and the nine levels of people in the *Meditation Sutra* is basically one of a 'combined' versus an 'expanded' mode of classification." It should be clearly understood that the Nembutsu practice is proper for each of the nine levels of people. How does one know this? The Nembutsu practice is found in all of the three classes; how then can it be absent in the nine levels? For this reason it is said in the *Collection on the Essentials for Rebirth*:

> One might ask, "Which one of the nine levels of people should adopt the practice of the Nembutsu?" The answer is that if one practices it in the manner expounded [in the sutra], then it is logical to assume that it is the highest level of the superior class. For people are to be divided into the nine levels according to their superior or inferior capacities. Although only one part of the practices of the nine levels of people is expounded in the *Meditation Sutra*, there are, in actuality, countless practices.

It is for these reasons that one ought surely to know that the Nembutsu should be practiced by all nine levels of people.

According to the second interpretation, the aim of the *Meditation Sutra* is first to teach in a general manner the Contemplative and Distractive Practices in order to appeal universally to sentient beings of various capacities. Afterward, however, it states that one should abandon the Good Practices for Contemplative and Distracted [People] and take refuge in the single practice of the Nembutsu. This is the meaning of the passage, "You should hold firmly to these words," and so on. The meaning of this quotation will be explained in detail below. It is for these reasons that you should surely understand that the practice that is proper to all nine classes of people is the Nembutsu alone.

8a

Chapter V

The Benefits of the Nembutsu

Passages on the Benefits of the Nembutsu

In the second volume of the *Sutra of Immeasurable Life* it is said:

> The Buddha said to Maitreya that if sentient beings should hear the Name of the Buddha and, happy enough to dance for joy, should think of him even once, then they could be sure of attaining the great benefit of acquiring unsurpassable merit.

In Shan-tao's *Hymns in Praise of Rebirth* it is said:

> If sentient beings should hear
> The Name of Amida
> And rejoice even for a moment of thought
> They will all attain Rebirth.

Someone might ask, "According to the above passage on the three classes of people, the awakening of the Bodhi mind and other virtues are mentioned in addition to the Nembutsu. Why then do these scriptures praise the merits of the Nembutsu alone and not these other virtues as well?" I should in answer say that the Holy Intention is difficult to fathom and its meaning surely profound. Let us listen briefly to what Shan-tao says on this matter. He declared that although originally the Buddha immediately wished to expound the practice of the Nembutsu alone, nevertheless, taking

53

into account the differing capacities of sentient beings, as a tentative measure he expounded the awakening of the Bodhi mind and other manifold practices, thus drawing distinctions between the relative shallowness or depth of the three classes of people. Now, however, he has cast aside the manifold practices and no longer praises them. Since they have been laid aside, they need not be discussed. On the other hand, the one practice of the Nembutsu alone has already been chosen and is praised. We should ponder and consider this well.

If the three classes are considered in terms of the Nembutsu, there are two implications: (1) the three classes of people are distinguished according to the shallowness or the depth of their contemplation [of Amida], and (2) the three classes are divided according to whether their Nembutsus are many or few.

If the Nembutsu practitioners are classified on the basis of shallowness or depth, then as was stated above, "If one practices it in the manner expounded in the sutra, then unquestionably the answer will be the highest level of the superior class."

Next, regarding the classification of men according to whether their Nembutsus be many or few, in the passage on the lower class the numberings of "ten times" or "even once" have already appeared. As regards the other two, the middle and superior classes, the number of Nembutsus should be increased accordingly. In *The Dharma Gate of Contemplation* it is said:

> Every day one should recite the Nembutsu ten thousand times, and also at the proper times one should honor and praise the adornments of the Pure Land. One should apply oneself to this with great zeal. Those who are able to recite it thirty, sixty, or a hundred thousand times all belong to the highest level of the superior class.

One ought surely to know that reciting the Nembutsu more than thirty thousand times belongs to the practice of the highest level of the superior class. It is now clear that classes and levels [of people] are distinguished in accord with the greater or lesser number of their Nembutsus.

Now let us consider the "one Nembutsu." It refers on the one hand to the "one Nembutsu" mentioned in the above passage concerning the fulfillment of the Vow of the Nembutsu. It refers also to the "one Nembutsu" that is spoken of in the passage concerning the lower class; less than thirty thousand times is practice ranking below the superior. Although in the passage on the fulfillment of the Vow "one Nembutsu" was also spoken of, the great benefit of its merits has not yet been explained. Likewise, the "one Nem- 8b butsu" was mentioned in the passage on the lower class, but the great benefit of its merits was not explained.

When expounding this "one Nembutsu" the *Sutra* [*of Immeasurable Life*] declares its great benefit and praises it as unsurpassed. It should be understood that this is intended to include the various examples of "one Nembutsu" referred to earlier.

"Great benefit" is the opposite of "small benefit." Hence, the manifold practices of awakening the Bodhi mind and the rest are of small benefit. "Even one Nembutsu" is of great benefit. Further, the words "unsurpassed merits" are the opposite of "merits that can be surpassed." The remaining practices, then, are regarded as surpassable.

The Nembutsu is said to be unsurpassed. It has already been declared that "one Nembutsu" contains an unsurpassed quantity of merits. Hence, it ought to be clearly understood that ten Nembutsus contain ten unsurpassed quantities of merit, that a hundred Nembutsus contain a hundred, and a thousand contain a thousand unsurpassed quantities of merit.

In this manner, merits evolve and expand from few to many. If the Nembutsus become as great in number as the sands of the Ganges, then the unsurpassed quantities of merit too will be as numerous as the sands of the Ganges. One should surely understand it in this manner. If this is the case, then why should people who desire Rebirth abandon the Nembutsu with its unsurpassed great benefits and strive to perform the other practices with their small and surpassable benefits?

Chapter VI

The Nembutsu Alone Will Remain

Passages Relating That the Nembutsu Alone Will Remain [in the World] after the Ten Thousand Year Age of the Decadence of the Dharma, When All of the Other Practices Have Disappeared

It is said in the second volume of the *Sutra of Immeasurable Life*:

> In the future world, when the way of sutras has disappeared, I, pitying [sentient beings] with merciful compassion, shall as a special exception cause this sutra alone to remain for yet another hundred years. Then the sentient beings who encounter this sutra will, if in their hearts they so desire, all be able to attain the other shore.

Someone might ask, "In the sutra it is said, 'I . . . shall . . . cause this sutra alone to remain for yet another hundred years.' Nowhere is it stated, 'I shall cause the Nembutsu alone to endure for yet another hundred years.' So why do you now say, 'the Nembutsu alone'?" I would answer that what is expressed in this sutra primarily concerns the Nembutsu. This implication was expounded above and so it would be improper to repeat it. Shan-tao, Huai-kan, and Eishin also expressed the same notion. Hence the sutra's promise that "it will remain" means that the Nembutsu will remain. Moreover, even though the phrase "awakening the Bodhi mind" appears in this sutra, it does not teach the manner of its practice. Further, even though the phrase "observing the precepts" also appears in this sutra, it does not teach the manner of its practice. The manner of practice for the awakening of the Bodhi mind is treated at length in the *Bodhi Mind Sutra* and elsewhere. But if this sutra will already have disappeared, then how could anyone actually achieve in practice the awakening of the Bodhi mind? Similarly, the manner of "observing the precepts" is expounded at length in the Mahayana and Hinayana Vinaya texts. But if the Vinaya texts have already disappeared, then how could anyone practice "observing the precepts"? One can see by this that the same applies to other manifold practices. Thus the Master Shantao, in his *Hymns in Praise of Rebirth*, explained the above passage as follows:

8c   The Three Treasures will disappear in ten thousand
         years,
      But this sutra will endure for yet another hundred years.
      During that interval, everyone who hears this sutra and
         thinks [of Amida] even once,
      Will certainly be able to attain Rebirth in that Land.

Briefly, there are four implied meanings by which this passage can be properly understood: (1) There are two teachings, the Holy Path and the Pure Land. One will remain after the other has passed away. (2) There are the Two Teachings, one concerning the Pure Lands of the ten directions and one concerning the Pure Land of the West. One will remain after the other has passed away. (3) There are two teachings, one of the Tuṣita heaven [of Maitreya] and one of the Pure Land of the West. One will remain after the other has passed away. (4) There are two types of practice, the Nembutsu and the manifold practices. One of these will remain after the other has passed away.

Regarding the first implied meaning concerning the Holy Path and the Pure Land, the passage indicates that the many sutras in the Gateway of the Holy Path will pass away first. That is why it says, "When the way of the sutras has disappeared . . ." But only this sutra, [the *Sutra of Immeasurable Life*] of the Pure Land Gateway will remain. That is why it says it will "endure for yet another hundred years." It should certainly be understood that our karmic relationship with the Holy Path is shallow and thin, whereas our karmic relationship with the Pure Land is deep and strong.

Regarding the second implied meaning, concerning the Pure Lands of the ten directions and the Western Pure Land, the passage indicates that the many teachings about Rebirth in the Pure Lands of the ten directions will pass away first. That is why it says, "When the way of the sutras has disappeared . . ." Only that sutra that expounds Rebirth in the Western Pure Land will remain. Thus the passage says that it will "endure for yet another hundred years." One should certainly realize that our karmic relationship with the Pure Lands of the ten directions is shallow and thin, whereas that with the Pure Land is deep and strong.

Regarding the third implied meaning concerning the Tuṣita Heaven and the Western Paradise, the passage indicates that the various teachings about ascent and Rebirth into the Tuṣita heaven as presented in the *Sutra on Ascent and Rebirth*, the *Sutra of Meditation on Mind*, and the like, will disappear first. That is why it says, "When the way of the sutras has disappeared . . ." Only that sutra that expounds Rebirth in the Western Paradise will remain. That is why it says that it will "endure for yet another hundred years." Although the Tuṣita heaven is near, our karmic relationship to it is shallow. On the other hand, although the Land of Supreme Bliss is far away, our affinity for it is deep.

Regarding the fourth implied meaning concerning the Nembutsu and the manifold practices, the passage implies that the many teachings concerning the manifold practices leading to Rebirth will pass away first. That is why it says, "When the way of the sutras has disappeared . . ." Only that sutra that expounds Rebirth through the Nembutsu will endure. Hence, the passage says that it will "endure for yet another hundred years." And so it is that our karmic relationship with Rebirth through the manifold practices is very shallow whereas that with Rebirth through the Nembutsu is extremely deep. In addition to this, those who have a karmic relationship with Rebirth through the manifold practices are few, whereas those with a relationship to Rebirth through the Nembutsu are many. Further, Rebirth through the manifold practices is limited to the ten-thousand-year Age of the Dharma's Decadence, which is now at hand, while Rebirth through the Nembutsu will be of benefit for a hundred years after the extinction of the Dharma, which is still far in the future.

One might ask, "Above it was said, 'I, pitying [sentient beings] with merciful compassion, will as a special exception cause this sutra to endure for yet another hundred years.' If Śākyamuni, out of merciful compassion, should cause the teaching of a sutra to endure, why would he not cause all the other teachings and all the other sutras to endure? Why would he choose that this sutra alone would remain and not the others?" I would in answer say that if he would choose any sutra at all and cause it to remain, this same problem of choosing only one sutra could not be avoided. But he did in fact declare that only this sutra as a special exception will endure. Does not this fact in itself contain a profound meaning?

9a   If we rely on the opinion of the Master Shan-tao, we find that already in this sutra, Amida Tathāgata's Original Vow of Rebirth through the Nembutsu is expounded. Śākyamuni, in his merciful compassion, in order that the Nembutsu might endure, as a special exception, caused this sutra to remain. The other sutras do not teach Amida Tathāgata's Original Vow of Rebirth through the Nembutsu. That is why Śākyamuni compassionately did not cause them to remain. Although generally speaking all Forty-eight Vows are Original Vows, the Nembutsu was specially prescribed as the means for Rebirth. Therefore, Shan-tao said in the *Commentary*:

> The Universal Vows are many,
> As many as forty-eight,
> But the Nembutsu alone was revealed
> As the [practice with] greatest karmic relationship.
> If anyone often thinks of the Buddha,
> The Buddha in turn will think of him.

60

If one concentrates on the Buddha with his whole heart,
The Buddha in turn will recognize him.

Therefore from the above it should be clear that the Vow of Rebirth
through the Nembutsu was already long ago made king among the
Forty-eight Original Vows. For this reason Śākyamuni—out of compassion and as a special exception—ordained that this sutra will
endure for yet another hundred years. Thus in the *Meditation Sutra*
Śākyamuni did not specially entrust [to Ānanda] the Contemplative and Distractive Practices but rather specially entrusted the
practice of the Nembutsu alone. That is to say, it was because it
accorded with the Vows of the Buddha that the one practice of the
Nembutsu was transmitted [to Ānanda].

It may be asked, "The above may well be the reason why the
Nembutsu will endure for an extra hundred years, but is it not
perhaps the case that this practice is suited only to people of that
period? Or is it also suited to people of the Ages of the Right Dharma
and the Semblance of the Dharma, as well as that of the Decadence of the Dharma?" I should in answer say that it is suitable
for all three ages. But one ought certainly to understand that although Śākyamuni mentioned that last period only, he meant to
urge that we should practice it now.

Chapter VII

The Light of Amida Envelops the Nembutsu Practitioners

Passages Revealing That the Light of Amida Does Not Envelop Those Who Engage in the Other Practices but Only Those Who Practice the Nembutsu

It is said in the *Meditation Sutra*:

> The Buddha of Immeasurable Life has the eighty-four thousand major marks of physical excellence, each one of which has the eighty-four thousand minor marks; each minor mark also has eighty-four thousand rays of light. Each ray of light shines throughout the ten directions of the universe. They all envelop the sentient beings who practice the Nembutsu and never abandon them.

In the *Commentary* on the same sutra it is said:

> The passage beginning with "The Buddha of Immeasurable Life" and ending with "envelop and never abandon them," clearly shows that if one meditates on the special characteristics of Amida's body, one finds that his light benefits those who have a close karmic relationship with him. Thus it explains five points. First, it clarifies whether the major

marks of excellence are many or few; second, whether the minor marks of excellence are many or few; third, whether the rays of light are few or many; fourth, whether the light reaches far or near [worlds]; and fifth, it reveals that wherever the light reaches people enjoy the benefits of its embrace. One might ask, "If people engage in various practices and are careful to turn over their merits toward Rebirth, then they all can attain it; then why does the light of the Buddha, which shines everywhere, envelop only those who practice the Nembutsu? What is the meaning of this?"

I should in answer say that there are three meanings. The first clarifies the intimate karmic relation [with Amida]. When sentient beings awaken themselves to practice and always utter the Name of the Buddha, the Buddha will hear them. When they constantly bow in reverence to the Buddha, the Buddha will see them. When they continually think of the Buddha, the Buddha will know them. When sentient beings remember the Buddha, the Buddha will also remember them. The three karmic acts of the Buddha and those of sentient beings are not separate from each other. That is why this is called the intimate relation.

9b

The second meaning clarifies the close karmic relation. When sentient beings desire to see the Buddha, he, in response to this desire, will appear before their very eyes. Hence, this is called the close karmic relation.

The third clarifies the superior karmic relation. Sentient beings who utter the Nembutsu are rid of the accumulated sins of many kalpas. When they are at the point of death, the Buddha together with the holy assembly will come in person to welcome them. The evil karma cannot obstruct their coming. That is why it is called the superior karmic relation.

The remaining manifold practices, even though they are called "good," cannot even be compared with the Nembutsu. That is why in many passages of various sutras the virtues of the Nembutsu are widely praised. For example, in the Forty-eight Vows of the *Sutra of Immeasurable Life* it is explained that only by meditating wholeheartedly on the Name of Amida can one be reborn. Further, in the *Amida Sutra* one reads that by meditating wholeheartedly from one to seven days on the Name of Amida one can attain Rebirth. And also, the testimony of the many Buddhas of the ten directions as countless as the sands of the Ganges is not false. Also, in the passage of the [*Meditation*] *Sutra* concerning the Contemplative and Distractive Practices it is revealed that by simply meditating wholeheartedly on the Name, one can be reborn. There are numerous other examples like these. This ends the discussion of the Nembutsu Samādhi.

In the *Dharma Gate of Contemplation* it is said:

> Further, as was indicated above, each one of the rays of light emanating from Amida's bodily marks, and so forth, shine everywhere throughout the ten directions of the universe, but the light of that Buddha's mind and heart envelops only those sentient beings who meditate wholeheartedly on Amida Buddha, embracing and protecting them and never abandoning them. Nothing is said about it enveloping those who engage in any of the remaining Miscellaneous Practices.

One might ask, "What meaning is there in the fact that the Buddha's light shines only on practitioners of the Nembutsu but does not envelop those who perform other practices?" I should in answer say that according to my interpretation there are two meanings. The first pertains to the three karmic relations, such as the intimate karmic relation shown in the above quotation. The second pertains to the Original Vow. Because the other practices are not in accord with the Original Vow, this light does not envelop them. But it does envelop the Nembutsu because it is in accord with the Original Vow. For this reason Master Shan-tao says in the *Hymns for the Six Periods in Praise of Rebirth*:

The color of Amida's body is like that of a luminous
golden mountain.
The light from his major and minor marks illumines the
ten directions.
Only those who utter the Nembutsu are enveloped in his
light.
One should surely realize that the Original Vow is the
most powerful.

Again, in the passage already quoted, it is stated, "The remaining
manifold practices, even though they are called 'good,' cannot even
be compared with the Nembutsu." I would interpret this as follows: This is a comparison with regard to the various practices of
the Pure Land Gateway. The Nembutsu is the refined practice
which was long ago adopted from among twenty-one billion practices. The manifold practices are the coarse ones which were among
the twenty-one billion already rejected. This is why it is said that
they "cannot even be compared [with the Nembutsu]." Further,
the Nembutsu is the practice of the Original Vow. The manifold
practices are not. That is why it is said that they "cannot even be
compared [with the Nembutsu]."

9c

Chapter VIII

The Three Minds

Passages Showing That Those Who Practice the
Nembutsu Should Certainly Possess the Three Minds

In the *Meditation Sutra* it is said:

> If there are sentient beings who desire Rebirth in that Land,
> they must awaken in themselves the three kinds of mind.
> Then they will be reborn. What are the Three Minds? The
> first is the sincere mind; the second is the deep mind; the
> third is the mind that is determined to transfer all merits
> toward Rebirth. If one possesses these Three Minds, one
> will unquestionably attain Rebirth in that Land.

In the *Commentary* on the same sutra it is said:

> In regard to the first mind mentioned in the sutra, the sin-
> cere mind (*lit.* "utmost sincere mind"), "utmost" means
> "true[ly]," and "sincere" means "authentic." This word is
> intended to make it clear that the understanding and prac-
> tice that all sentient beings achieve through physical, vo-
> cal, and mental activities must necessarily be realized and
> accomplished with a "truly authentic" mind. One should
> not outwardly appear to be wise, good, and diligent while
> inwardly nourishing falsehood. Human beings' greed, anger,
> evil, falsehood, deceit, and pretension have a hundred facets.

Their evil nature is as difficult to combat as snakes and scorpions. Even though they might practice the three karmic actions, these are said to be good practices mixed with poison. And so they should be called vain and false practice; they cannot be called "truly authentic" acts. Even if people should possess in their practice such a "peaceful mind"; even though they drive their bodies and minds, and run about engaged in practice all hours of the day and night with the same compulsive haste as they would brush live coals from their heads; all of this should still be called good mixed with poison.

Even if they should wish to be reborn in that Buddha's Pure Land by transferring [the merits of] these practices mixed with poison, it would certainly be impossible. The reason for this is that when Amida Buddha, while still in the preparatory stage, performed the practices of a Bodhisattva, he carried out in every thought, and at every moment, all of the three karmic actions with a truly authentic mind. All his practice, whether it involved acts of compassion toward others, or striving for his own Enlightenment, was truly authentic.

Further, there are two kinds of true authenticity; the first is being true and authentic in regard to that which benefits oneself; the second is being truly authentic with respect to that which benefits others. And also within that which benefits oneself there are two more varieties of true authenticity.

As to the first, people with a truly authentic mind and heart subdue or cast out of themselves and others manifold evils of the defiled lands. They must resolve, whether they are walking, standing still, sitting, or lying down, personally to subdue and cast out the manifold evils, just as all Bodhisattvas do. As to the second, with a truly authentic mind they diligently foster in themselves and others the good practices of both ordinary and holy persons. With a truly authentic mind they employ vocal practice to praise

Amida and his two principal and dependent recompenses: Amida himself and his Land. Also, with a truly authentic mind they employ vocal practice to condemn and destroy the painful and evil things of the two principal and dependent evil recompenses: the three worlds and the six realms. They also praise the three karmic actions or good practices done by all sentient beings. They remain respectful but keep their distance from those whose practices are not good, and they never condone their actions.

Further, with a truly authentic mind and heart they employ physical practice, joining their palms, doing reverence, and making offerings of the four things to Amida Buddha and to his two principal and dependent recompenses. Also, with a truly authentic mind they employ physical practice to hold in contempt, despise, and cast out of themselves and others the two principal and dependent evil recompenses, that is, samsara and the three worlds. Further, with a truly authentic mind they employ mental practice to think on, contemplate, and remember Amida Buddha and his two principal and dependent recompenses, as though they were before their very eyes. Likewise, with a truly authentic mind they use mental practice to despise and reject in themselves and others the two principal and dependent evil recompenses: samsara and the three worlds. By all means such people must certainly reject with a truly authentic mind any improper practice of the three karmic actions; but if an opportunity for genuinely good practice of the three karmic actions presents itself, they should perform them with a truly authentic mind. Whether concerning matters of the inner mind or of outer appearances, whether of clearly evident or of darkly obscure matters, they should at all costs be truly authentic in everything. [Such are the practices that the sutra] calls "the sincere mind."

The second is the deep mind. The deep mind is the mind of deep faith. It, too, has two aspects. The first is firmly and

10a

deeply to believe that now in this present body one is an
ordinary sinful human being who has been for countless
kalpas always sunk tumbling in the stream of cyclic births
and deaths, unable to find the karmic conditions for escape.
The second aspect is firmly and deeply to believe that Amida
Buddha's Forty-eight Vows enfold sentient beings in their
embrace and that those who without doubt or apprehen-
sion entrust themselves to the power of these Vows will certainly attain Rebirth.

Further, [deep faith] is firmly and deeply to believe that
Śākyamuni Buddha in the *Meditation Sutra* expounded the
three meritorious practices, the nine classes of people, and
the Two Good—Contemplative and Distractive—Practices;
that he gave witness and praise to the principal and dependent recompenses of [Amida] Buddha and urged men to
aspire joyfully towards that Land.

It is firmly and deeply to believe that in the *Amida Sutra*
the many Buddhas of the ten directions, as numberless as
the sands of the Ganges, testify that all ordinary people
can assuredly attain Rebirth; and that they encourage them
to seek it.

Moreover, deep faith is to wish and to request that all
practitioners single-mindedly believe only in the Buddha's
words and that they, without concern for their physical well-
being, resolutely rely on this practice. It is to cast aside that
which the Buddha would have one cast aside, to practice
that which the Buddha would have one practice, and to leave
behind that which the Buddha would have one leave behind. This is known as following the Buddha's teaching and
being in accord with the Buddha's intention; it is known as
following the Buddha's Vow. It is called being a true disciple of the Buddha.

Furthermore, I assure all practitioners that those who
practice with deep faith according to this sutra will surely
not lead sentient beings astray. Why is this so? Because the
Buddha is one who has perfect great compassion and his

words are true. Except for the Buddha, there is no one who is perfect in wisdom and practice. The others still remain in the stage of learning. They have yet to remove the two actual and residual obstacles, and their vows have yet to be completely fulfilled. Even if they—whether ordinary or Holy People— ponder on the import of the many Buddhas' teachings, they cannot reach a thorough understanding of them. Even if they do gain clear and correct understanding, they still by all means need the witness of the Buddha in order to be certain.

If their understanding is in accord with the Buddha's Mind, he will give his approval saying, "So it is, so it is." If it is not in accord with the Buddha's Mind, he will say, "Your words do not accord with my teaching." [When the Buddha gives] no sign, then [those teachings] are like words that are neither good nor evil; they are neither beneficial nor profitable. But if the Buddha gives his approval to something, then it is in accord with his authentic teachings. Every word that the Buddha expounds expresses his authentic teaching, his authentic meaning, his authentic practice, his authentic understanding, his authentic karmic activity, and his authentic wisdom. How can any other being, be it a Bodhisattva, a human being, or a *deva*, decide on the truth or falsehood of a Buddha's words, be they few or many? If a Buddha teaches something, it is the full teaching; what Bodhisattvas and the like teach are known to be teachings that are not yet full. One ought surely to understand this. It is for this reason that I now urge all those who have karmic affinity with Rebirth to cultivate deep faith in the Buddha's words alone and with single-minded concentration to put them into practice. One should not believe the teachings of Bodhisattvas and others that are not in accord with the Buddha's intent, should not sow doubt, should not become confused and embrace delusion, and should not forfeit the great benefits of attaining Rebirth.

The deep mind or deep faith involves a decisive determination of one's mind to practice in accord with the

10b

[Buddha's] teachings; it involves forever setting aside all doubts and falsehoods and never retreating or wavering in the face of all the other interpretations, practices, different teachings, different views, and different contentions.

One might ask, "The wisdom of the ordinary man is shallow and his delusions and the obstructions in his way are deep-rooted. Suppose we meet a person whose understanding and practice differ from ours and who attempts to hinder us by proving with passages from many sutras and treatises that no sinful ordinary man is able to attain Rebirth. How might we refute such a person's argument and so vindicate our own deep faith and then decisively march straight ahead without discouragement or retreat?"

I should answer that if a practitioner should meet such a one who tries to prove with passages from the many sutras and treatises that no sinful ordinary person can attain Rebirth, he or she should reply, "Even though you come to me with the sutras and treatises and say they prove that I cannot be reborn, my own understanding will certainly suffer no harm from your attacks. The reason is not that I do not have faith in the many sutras and treatises, for I reverently believe in all of them. The Buddha, however, expounded these sutras at differing times and in different places to sentient beings of differing capacities in order to bless them with differing benefits. The occasions when the Buddha expounded these sutras were not the same as those when he expounded the *Meditation*, the *Amida*, and other Pure Land sutras.

"Thus he revealed these teachings in order to accommodate the varying capacities of his hearers at various times. That is to say, he revealed doctrines and practices that were generally appropriate for human beings, *deva*s, and Bodhisattvas. But now he expounds the *Meditation Sutra*'s two good practices: the Contemplative and the Distractive. He expounded these only for Vaidehī and for all the ordinary men of the Five Defilements and the five grievous sufferings, who live in the period after the Buddha departed from this world. This testifies that all ordinary men can attain Rebirth. For this reason I now rely single-mindedly upon this teaching of the Buddha and engage in determined practice. And so even if a hundred thousand trillion men like you were to say that I could not be reborn, I would nevertheless continue to strengthen and perfect the faith in Rebirth which is in my heart."

Furthermore, the practitioner should turn again to such a person and teach him, saying, "Listen well, and I will further reveal to you the decisive quality of our faith. Even if there would be Bodhisattvas who have not yet reached the first stage, Arhats, and *Pratyekabuddhas*—whether one or many, or even so numerous as to fill the ten directions— who would quote sutras and treatises to prove that I will not be reborn, still not a single doubtful thought would arise in my mind. Rather, I would strive to strengthen and perfect the purity of my faith. Why should I do this? Because the Buddha's words are the decisive, perfect, and full teaching; absolutely nothing can destroy them."

Practitioners, you should listen carefully to this. Even if Bodhisattvas who have reached from the first to the tenth stage, whether one or many or even numerous enough to fill all of the ten directions, would all say in one voice that it is absolutely false that Śākyamuni singled out and praised Amida, scorning the three worlds and six realms, false that he encouraged sentient beings to practice the Nembutsu wholeheartedly, and false that he said that even by engaging in the other good practices one could, after the death of this present body, unquestionably be able to be reborn in that Land, still, one should not believe such falsities or rely on them. And even if I should hear such words, not a single doubt would arise in my heart. Rather, I would strengthen and perfect the purity of my faith.

10c

Why should I do this? Because the Buddha's words reveal the true, authentic, decisive, and full Teaching. Since the Buddha embodies authentic wisdom, authentic understanding, authentic insight, and authentic Enlightenment, he does not speak with an uncertain mind. Further, his words cannot be destroyed by the differing views and interpretations of all these Bodhisattvas. If they were truly Bodhisattvas, they would not differ from the Buddha's teaching.

The practitioner must further clearly understand that I would not doubt even if Buddhas in their transformation or recompense bodies—whether one or many or even so numerous as to fill the worlds of the ten directions, each one radiating light and stretching forth his tongue to encompass all the worlds of the ten directions—should each declare: "It is false. It is absolutely not true that Śākyamuni's teachings praised Amida and urged all ordinary men to practice the Nembutsu wholeheartedly, and to perform other good acts so that by transferring the merits of such practices they could be reborn in the Pure Land. These notions are false; certainly such things cannot be." Even if I were to listen to the explanations of such Buddhas, still not a single notion of doubt or retreat—which might cause me to fear that I might fail to attain Rebirth in that Buddha's Land—would arise in my heart.

Why is this so? Because one Buddha is all the Buddhas. Their knowledge, their understanding and practice, their Enlightenment, the fruits they have gained through practice, and their great compassion are all identical. There is not the slightest difference among them. For this reason, what one Buddha determines is the same as that which all the Buddhas determine.

This is like the previous Buddha's decision to prohibit the ten evils: not to kill living beings, and so forth. After that decision, such sins are not to be committed or performed at all; such observances have come to be called the ten goods, the Ten [Good] Practices, or the practice that accords with the six *pāramitā*s. If a succeeding Buddha should later appear in the world, is it conceivable that he would reverse this and have one perform the ten evils instead of the ten goods?

By the same token it is clear that there is no discrepancy between either the words or the deeds of the many Buddhas. If then Śākyamuni encouraged all ordinary people to engage wholeheartedly and continually in the one practice of the Nembutsu while in their present bodies, and if he assured them that after their lives had ended they would surely be reborn in that Land, then all the Buddhas of the ten directions would equally praise, equally encourage, and equally confirm this.

Why is this so? Because they all form a single body of great compassion. The teaching of one Buddha is the teaching of all the Buddhas. The teaching of all the Buddhas is the teaching of a single Buddha.

Thus, in the *Amida Sutra* it is taught that Śākyamuni praised and extolled the various adornments of the Land of Supreme Bliss. Further, he encouraged all ordinary men by saying that if they contemplate Amida's Name single-mindedly and wholeheartedly from one to seven days, they can certainly attain Rebirth. In a subsequent passage the sutra also says, "In each world of the ten directions there are Buddhas as countless as the sands of the Ganges. They all equally praise Śākyamuni who in the evil Age of the Five Defilements—an age when the world is evil, sentient beings are evil, views are evil, passions are evil, and when vice and disbelief abound—singled out and extolled Amida's Name and encouraged sentient beings by declaring that those who utter that Name would certainly be able to be reborn." Here then is proof that what has been said is true. 11a

Further, all of the Buddhas in the worlds of the ten directions, fearing that sentient beings would not believe what the Buddha Śākyamuni had said, have together with one mind simultaneously stretched forth their tongues and covered with them the three thousand worlds, declaring with sincere and authentic words, "All you sentient beings should without question believe in those things that Śākyamuni taught, praised, and witnessed. There is absolutely no doubt that all ordinary men, irrespective of whether their sins or virtuous acts be great or small, or whether the time [they devote to practice] be long or short—can surely be reborn if they single-mindedly and wholeheartedly contemplate the Name of Amida, for at most a hundred years or at least from one to seven days." In this manner, that which one Buddha taught, all the other Buddhas together have earnestly borne witness. This is known as "establishment of faith in a person."

Next, let us consider "establishment of faith in practice." This involves the two kinds of practice. One is Right Practice and the other, Miscellaneous Practice. (These are the same as the two kinds of practice treated in the second chapter. To avoid unnecessary repetition they will not be recited again here. Please refer to those passages if you wish to ascertain their meaning.) [Hōnen's own comment]

The third, which is known as the mind that desires to transfer [merits], is the mind that awakens the desire for Rebirth in that Land. It does this by [transferring] the good deeds—worldly and world-transcending—achieved by [one's own] physical, vocal, and mental practices of the past and the present, and by taking appropriate delight in the good deeds—worldly and world-transcending—achieved by the physical, vocal, and mental practices of all other ordinary and Holy Beings: [that is] by transferring [toward Rebirth] all [the merits] of the good deeds achieved by oneself and others with a mind of true and profound faith. It is for this reason that it is called the mind desiring to transfer [all merits toward Rebirth].

Those who transfer [merits] and awaken this desire to be reborn should be convinced that they can indeed attain

Rebirth by such a determined transferring if it is done with a truly authentic mind. This mind, because of its deep faith, is as hard as a diamond; it will not be perturbed or destroyed by those who hold to different views, studies, understandings, and practices. Go straight forward, decisively and wholeheartedly. Do not listen to the words of those other men, for with them comes vacillation from which weakness is born in the heart. If one begins to look hither and yon, one falls into the realms of the evil world, and loses the great benefit of Rebirth.

Someone might ask what he or she should do if those who have different understandings and practices and who hold various mistaken ideas come and create confusion by expressing various doubts and criticisms, teaching that one cannot attain Rebirth. Or what if they should say, "You and all other sentient beings have already, for countless kalpas up to your present lives, committed sins against all kinds of ordinary and Holy People through evil karma of body, speech, and mind. You have committed the ten evils, the five deadly sins, the four grievous deeds; you have abused the Dharma, fallen into the sin of the *icchantika*s, broken the precepts, offended against proper teaching, and committed other sinful deeds. Such terrible sins have not yet been erased. They still bind you to the evil realms of the three worlds. How then can you in a single lifetime of performing the meritorious practices and the Nembutsu enter into the Land of No Defilement and No Birth [or Death], abiding long in the Stage of Non-Retrogression?"

I should answer that the teachings and practices of all the Buddhas are more numerous than there are specks of dust and grains of sand. Equally varied are the potentialities and karmic conditions of sentient beings. For example, there are things that men and women in the world can see and believe with their eyes: light banishes darkness, the sky arches over all things, the earth can support and nourish living things, water both enlivens and irrigates, and fire

11b

both produces and destroys. Such things are all said to illustrate the mutual relationship of all things. As our eyes
can see, their variety is infinite.

Why then should not the mysterious power of the
Buddha's Dharma bring many different kinds of benefits?
And accordingly, when a man leaves one gateway, he leaves
one gateway of the deluding passions; and whenever he enters a gateway, he enters the gateway of emancipating wisdom. In this way, every person should begin practice in
accord with his karmic condition and so seek his own emancipation. Why then do you hinder and confuse me with practices that do not accord with my karmic affinities? The
practice that I love is the one with which I have karmic
affinity. However, it is not the one you seek. The one you
love is the practice with which you have karmic affinity,
but it is not the one I seek. For this reason, if each of us
carries out the practice that accords with his own desires
we shall all surely attain emancipation quickly.

All practitioners should be aware that if one wishes to
study doctrines, one could study any of them freely, from those
teachings concerning the realm of ordinary men to those concerning the realm of the Holy Persons and so on, all the
way up to the fruit of Buddhahood itself. If, however, one
intends to study practice, one should surely rely on the
Dharma with which one has affinity. It is thus that one can
gain the greatest benefit with the least amount of effort.

Now I should like to say something for the sake of everyone who desires Rebirth. I wish to relate a parable in
order to protect the faith in their minds and defend it from
foreign and heretical views. What is this?

Imagine a man intending to travel hundreds and thousands of miles to the West. Unexpectedly he comes upon
two rivers blocking the roadway. The one to the south is a
river of fire while the one to the north is of water. Each is a
hundred paces across, bottomless in depth, and stretches
endlessly to the north and south.

Exactly between the two streams of fire and water, there is a single white pathway about four or five inches wide which extends a hundred paces, from the eastern to the western shores. The waves of the water river surge over and submerge the path; the flames of the fire river rise up and sear it. Both the water and the fire continually surge over the passageway without rest.

The man, upon reaching this faraway deserted place, finds no one there except a large band of robbers and savage beasts. Seeing the man alone, they come racing after him intending to kill him. The man, fearing that death is imminent, turns and runs straight toward the West. But suddenly he sees those great rivers, and he says to himself, "I see no shore of these rivers, either to the north or south, but between them I see a single white path. It is extremely narrow. The distance between shores is not great, but how shall I cross? Surely I am doomed to die today! If I try to turn back, the band of robbers and savage beasts will close in for the kill. Certainly if I try to avoid them and flee to the north or south, there too savage beasts and poisonous insects will come racing to swarm upon me. If I go West and try to flee along the path, in all probability I shall fall into the stream of fire and water." At this point, his fear is too great to be described. He reflects further, "If I turn back, I shall die. If I stay here, I shall also die. If I go forward, I face the same fate. Since there is no escape from certain death, I had better go straight ahead over the narrow path that lies before me. Since a path exists, one must surely be able to cross over on it." 11c

While he is thinking in this way, from the eastern bank he suddenly hears someone encouraging him saying, "Oh traveller, simply make up your mind firmly to try to cross on this path and you will surely escape the pangs of death! If you linger here, you will surely die!" Then he hears someone else on the western shore calling and saying, "Oh traveller! Single-mindedly and with full concentration come straight forward. I can protect you! Do not worry about the horrors of falling into the fire or the water."

Hearing one voice urging him on and the other beckoning to him, he is able to steel his own body and mind properly, and he firmly resolves to try to cross over the path. He goes straight forward, allowing no doubt or uncertainty to arise in his mind. But after a step or two, he hears the gang of robbers on the eastern shore shouting, "Turn back, traveller! The path is dangerous! You cannot possibly pass over it. You will surely die! Our band means you no harm." But the traveller, even though he hears the voices calling him, does not go back or even glance behind him. Single-mindedly he moves straight forward concentrating on the path before him. Soon he reaches the western bank, free forever from all possible dangers. Then, in the company of good friends who have come to greet him, he rejoices greatly forever.

This is the parable. Now let me explain what it means. The eastern bank corresponds to our Saha world which is like a house on fire; the western bank is the Treasure Land of Supreme Bliss. The gang of robbers pretending to be kind-hearted and the pack of savage beasts represent the elements that make up all human beings: the six organs of sense, the six forms of consciousness and their six objects, the five aggregates, and the four elements. The barren and uninhabited marsh corresponds to [our condition] in which we are always tempted by evil companions and are never able to meet a true and good teacher.

The two rivers of water and of fire are like the greedy love that floods the hearts of all sentient beings and their hatred which burns like fire. The white path only four or five inches wide between the two rivers corresponds to the awakening of the pure mind that desires Rebirth in the midst of the evil passions of greed and anger. Because such greed and anger are strong, they are likened to fire and flood, whereas the good mind, being delicate, is like the white path. The surging waves that always wash over the path are like the covetousness that constantly arises to defile good hearts. The fire ceaselessly sending its flames burning over the path is like the anger and hatred of our hearts whose flames threaten to devour the Dharma treasure of merit and virtue.

The traveller turning directly to the West to cross over the path is like the practitioner turning straight to the West to transfer all his meritorious practice toward Rebirth. The fact that the traveller heard the voice on the eastern shore urging him to go forward and follow the path directly toward the West refers to people who, even after Śākyamuni has passed away, are able to follow the teaching of his Dharma, which still abides even though they no longer see the Buddha. The words of his teaching then are like the voice.

The traveler being called back by the band of robbers after taking only one or two steps shows that those followers of other doctrines and practices, or men with evil views who confuse others by their views and opinions, themselves commit sin and fall away from the path by teaching their views and opinions. By themselves committing sins, they regress and lose what little they had. The person on the western shore calling out to the traveller is Amida expressing his intent to save all beings through his Vow.

12a

The traveller's quick arrival on the western shore, joining his good friends and rejoicing in their company, is like sentient beings when they reach their final destination after having long been submerged in the sea of birth and death, deluded and bound by their evil passions, transmigrating for endless kalpas without knowing how to emancipate themselves. Favored by Śākyamuni who kindly encourages them by pointing to the West and turning them in that direction, and blessed with Amida Buddha's compassionate heart inviting and beckoning to them, they now trust in the intent of the two honorable ones without even taking notice of the two rivers of flame and water.

Remembering without fail the Original Vow, they take the path of the Vow's power. After death they can attain Rebirth in that Land, where they will meet the Buddha and where their joy will know no bounds.

Further, all the practitioners while engaging in their three forms of physical, vocal, and mental practice—whether walking or standing, sitting, or lying down, day or night—constantly believe and think in this manner. That is why this mind is called the mind that desires to transfer [all merits toward Rebirth].

"Transfer [all merits]" also means that after one has been reborn in that Land, he will attain great compassion and return to this world to teach and guide sentient beings. This too is a form of transferring.

When the Three Minds have been perfected, there is no practice that will remain unfulfilled. When both the desire and the practice have been perfected there will remain no reason why practitioners should not be reborn in the Pure Land. Further, these Three Minds also exist in the good practices. This should be carefully understood.

The *Hymns in Praise of Rebirth* says:

It may be asked, "I want to encourage people to attain Rebirth, but I do not understand how they can attain peace of heart, or what practices they should perform, or how they should perform them so that they can be certain of attaining Rebirth in that Land." I answer that according to the teachings of the *Meditation Sutra*, anyone who wishes to be certain that he or she will be reborn in that Land can attain such certainty if he or she possesses the Three Minds. What are these three? The first is the sincere mind. The physical practice [proper for attaining this mind] is bowing in reverence to the Buddha; its vocal practice is praising and extolling him, and its mental practice is wholeheartedly contemplating that Buddha. Whenever one performs these three practices, it is necessary that one do so with true authenticity. This is why it is called the "sincere" mind.

The second is the deep mind; that is, the mind of truly authentic faith that believes and knows that one is an ordinary being filled with deluding passions, that one's stock of meritorious deeds is shallow and meager, and that one has been, time and again, passing through cycles of birth and death in the three worlds, unable to flee the "burning house." One further believes and knows that Amida's Universal and Original Vow promises that if one utters the Name at least ten or at the very least one time, then one can certainly attain Rebirth. One allows not even a single doubtful thought to enter his mind. This is why it is called the deep mind.

The third is called the mind that desires to transfer [all merits toward Rebirth]. One desires Rebirth through the complete transfer of all the meritorious deeds which one accomplishes. That is why it is given the above name. If anyone possesses these Three Minds, without a doubt he or she will be reborn. If even one of these minds is lacking, he or she cannot be reborn. This matter is explained in detail in the *Meditation Sutra*. It should certainly be carefully noted.

In my opinion, the Three Minds in the above passages are of vital importance to practitioners. Why? Because in the *Meditation Sutra* it is stated that, "If one possesses these Three Minds, one will unquestionably attain Rebirth in that Land." We clearly know then that if one possesses these Three Minds one will certainly attain 12b Rebirth. This is explained [in *Hymns in Praise of Rebirth*], where it is said, "If even one of these minds is lacking, one will not be reborn." We clearly know then that one cannot lack even one of these. Therefore, the man who wishes to be reborn in the Land of Supreme Bliss should have fully realized these Three Minds.

Among these, that which is called the sincere mind is the mind that is truly authentic. Its characteristics are as described in the above passage. Thus in the passage, "outwardly appearing to be wise, good, and diligent while inwardly nourishing hypocrisy and falsehood," the word "outwardly" is the opposite of "inwardly." That is to say, one's outward aspect is out of accord with one's inner heart. In other words, outwardly one is wise, but inwardly one is a fool. "Wise" is the opposite of "foolish." In other words, outwardly a person is wise, but inwardly he is foolish. "Goodness" is the opposite of "evil," which is to say that outwardly a person is good while inwardly he is evil. "Diligence" stands in opposition to "laziness." This means that a person outwardly gives the appearance of diligence whereas inwardly his mind indulges in sloth.

If one were to turn around that which is exterior and put it inside, then surely one would possess what is essential for escaping from this world. In the passage, "inwardly nourishing falsehood," "inwardly" stands in opposition to "outwardly." That is to say, the inward heart is not in accord with the outward appearance; the interior is full of falsehood and the exterior seems authentic. "Falsehood" stands in opposition to "authenticity." The interior is full of falsehood while the exterior appears authentic. It says "falsehood" is the opposite of "truth." Hence, the passage means that the interior nourishes falsehood while the exterior appears to be true. If one were to turn around that which is interior and put it on the outside, then surely one would have what is essential for escaping from this world.

Next, regarding the deep mind, it is a mind of deep faith. One ought surely to know that it is through doubt that one is held fast within the house of samsara, while it is through faith that one can enter into the castle of nirvana. By thus establishing these two modes of the believing mind, the Rebirth of all nine classes of people is definitely assured. Further, the passage above that refers to "all the other interpretations, other practices, differing teachings, differing views" is speaking about the various interpretations, practices, and views of the Gateway of the Holy Path. The rest of the teachings refer to the Gateway of the Pure Land. You can see that these [truths] correspond to the passages [in Shan-tao's work]; and one should clearly know that Shan-tao's notions do not deviate from the teachings of the two pathways.

It is unnecessary to cite other explanations about the meaning of the mind that desires to transfer [all merits toward Rebirth]. Practitioners will surely already understand it well.

The Three Minds, if they are taken in a generalized manner, pervade all the modes of practice. But if they are taken in a special manner, they pertain to the practices that lead to Rebirth. Here, in presenting their general meaning I have included their special meanings as well. Their meaning is therefore universal. The practitioner should take special care not to be remiss in this regard.

Chapter IX

The Four Modes of Practice

*Passages Relating How Practitioners Should
Perform the Four Modes of Practice*

Shan-tao says in his *Hymns in Praise of Rebirth*:

Further, I wish to urge that you carry out the Four Modes
of Practice. What are these four? The first is the practice of
veneration: to venerate and reverence that Buddha as well
as all Holy Beings. For this reason it is called the practice
of veneration. When one never ceases it as long as one lives,
it is called the "long-term practice."

The second is called the exclusive practice. It is fervently
to utter the Name of that Buddha and devotedly to think of,
meditate on, wholeheartedly reverence, and praise that Buddha and all the other Holy Beings, but never to mix any other
practices with these. For this reason it is called the exclusive
practice. When one never ceases it throughout one's life, it is
called the "long-term practice."

The third is called the uninterrupted practice. It is to
continuously venerate, reverence, and recite his Name; it is
to praise him, to remember, and to contemplate him; and to
resolve to transfer [the merits of all practices toward Re-
birth]. It is to continue in these practices with total concentration and without interruption, allowing no room for other
practices to come and interfere. This is why it is called the

12c

uninterrupted practice. Further, there is no room for greed, anger, or the deluding passions to come and interfere. As soon as one commits such an offense, one should repent without allowing as much as a moment to pass, much less an hour or a day. To keep one's practice always pure is also called the uninterrupted practice. When one never ceases this throughout one's life, it is known as "long-term practice."

It is said in the *Essentials for Rebirth in the Western Paradise*:

One should perform only the Four Modes of Practice as the Right Practice. The first of these is the long-term practice: from the first awakening of aspiration for Enlightenment until the actual attainment of its realization, one should continually perform pure karmic deeds and never regress.

The second is the practice of veneration. It has five variations. The first is to venerate the Holy Persons with whom one has a karmic relationship; whether moving or standing still, sitting or lying down, one should never turn one's back on the West; and one should never blow one's nose, spit, or relieve oneself while facing the West.

The second variation is to venerate the images and holy scriptures of those with whom one has a karmic relationship. For the former, one should make images and pictures of Amida in the Western Paradise. If one should be unable to create many images, then only one Buddha and two Bodhisattvas are enough. As for venerating the holy scriptures, one should place the *Amida Sutra* and the other Pure Land sutras in a covering of the five colors and should read them oneself and teach them to others. One should enshrine these images and sutras in a room and there one should come six times a day and bow to them, repent one's sins before them, and, offering flowers and incense, specially esteem them.

The third is to venerate the good teachers with whom one has a karmic relationship. That is, if there is such a person who propagates the Pure Land teachings, even if he should be a hundred or a thousand miles away or more, still one should go to him, associate intimately with him, honor him, and make offerings to him.

One should also cultivate a respectful attitude toward all people who follow different teachings and should show deep respect for those who do not agree with one's views. Once one gives way to scorn and pride, the resulting sins will have no bounds. Therefore, one should show respect to all people and thus avoid creating obstacles which would impede one's practice.

The fourth is to respect the fellows with whom one shares a karmic relationship, that is, those who engage in the same practice. Even those who are not able to practice alone because of heavy karmic hindrances will certainly be able to practice well by relying on good friends. Thus they will be rescued from danger and saved from misfortune. Thus they are able to help and assist each other. People should deeply appreciate and esteem the good karmic relationship they have with their fellows.

The fifth is to reverence the Three Treasures. One should deeply reverence them whether taken together as a single entity or in their separate appearances. This matter will not be treated here in detail because people [of today], capable of only shallow effort, are unable to put its teachings into practice. Nevertheless, the Three Treasures in their represented forms produce great favorable karma in today's people of shallow understanding, and so I shall now briefly consider this matter.

As regards the Buddha treasure, his images should be carved in sandalwood, embroidered in brocade, made of plain materials, gilded with gold leaf, inlaid with precious stones, painted on silk, sculpted of stone, or molded from clay. One should give special reverence to the hallowed images. If anyone only briefly contemplates these forms, his sins will

13a vanish and his merit will increase. Whenever anyone suc-
cumbs to even the slightest pride, then his evil will increase
and his goodness will vanish. But contemplating the vener-
able images is equal to seeing the real Buddha.

The Dharma treasure is the teaching of the Three Vehicles expressed in words and phrases and flows out of the
Dharmadhātu. It is the cause that gives birth to our understanding. Therefore it deserves exceptional reverence. It is
the ground that gives rise to wisdom. One should copy the
sacred sutras. They should always be placed in consecrated
rooms, stored there in special boxes, and deeply revered.
Before chanting them, one should cleanse one's body and
hands. Regarding the Sangha treasure, one should awaken
in one's heart an equal respect for holy monks, Bodhisattvas,
and those who break the precepts. Do not give rise to proud
thoughts.

The third [of the Four Practices] is the uninterrupted
practice. This is to think of the Buddha always and to main-
tain a mind desirous of Rebirth. At all times one should
keep these things in mind. As an illustration let us imagine
a man [travelling in a foreign country] who is robbed and
who, being left in a mean and miserable state, is undergo-
ing various sufferings. Suddenly he thinks of his parents
and wants to rush back to his home but lacks the means to
equip himself for the journey. While he is in that foreign
land he broods day and night on his plight, and his pain is
too great to endure. Not even for a single moment can he
rid himself of the thoughts of his parents. At last he is able
to make the necessary preparations and actually returns to
his home. There he rejoices in being close to his father and
mother and is ecstatic with joy.

The same is true of the practitioner. The goodness of
his heart and mind has long ago been spoiled by deluding
passions, and the treasures of virtue and wisdom were all
lost. For long ages he has been swept along in the stream of

birth and death and is not free to control [his own destiny]. Always the servant of the devil king, he runs here and there among the six paths and suffers from torments of body and mind. But suddenly he encounters favorable karmic conditions; he hears that Amida, the compassionate father, will save the multitudes of beings, never deviating from his universal Vow. Day and night in utter astonishment, he cultivates the aspiration for Enlightenment and longs for Rebirth. In this manner, he diligently and untiringly thinks of the loving kindness of the Buddha. Until the end of his life he continually weighs and ponders these things in his heart.

The fourth is the Exclusive Practice. It is wholeheartedly to seek after the Land of Supreme Bliss while revering and thinking of Amida. One should not engage in the exercise or performance of any Miscellaneous Practices. The practice that one should engage in every day is the Nembutsu and the recitation of the sutras. Other practices should be cast aside.

I wish only to say that one should simply read the above passage concerning the Four Modes of Practice. I shall not explain it further for fear of making it complicated. However, in the first of the above quotations it was stated that there are four practices while only three were discussed. Has part of the text been omitted accidentally? Or is there a reason for such an omission? Without question no part of the text has been omitted. There is a deep meaning behind this. How do we know this? Of the Four Modes of Practice the first is the long-term practice, the second is the practice of earnest veneration, the third is the exclusive practice, and the fourth is the uninterrupted practice. The first, the long-term practice, pervades the other three. That is, if one were to cease the practice of earnest veneration, the exclusive practice, or the unremitting practice then one would be unable to bring any of these three practices to fulfillment.

13b

The long-term practice accompanies the other three in order to fulfill them. It pervades them and causes them to be carried out. For this reason, one finds at the end of the three passages concerning the practices the following words, "When one vows never to cease it until the end of one's life, this is called the 'long-term practice.'" If we look at the six *pāramitā*s we find an example of the same thing: the *pāramitā* of zeal pervades the other five *pāramitā*s.

Chapter X

Praise from the Transformation Buddha

Passages [that Relate How] Amida Buddha, When He Comes to Welcome [the Nembutsu Practitioners] in His Transformation Body, Does Not Praise Good Practices Such as Listening to the Sutras But Praises Only the Nembutsu

The *Meditation Sutra* says:

> There are some sentient beings who have done evil. Even though such persons may not have slandered the *Vaipulya* sutras, stupid persons like this commit very many evils but have no remorse. When such persons are about to die, should they meet a good teacher who praises the names of the Mahayana sutras in their twelve divisions, then, because they have heard the names of all these sutras, they will be freed from the extremely heavy evil karma accumulated over thousands of kalpas. Should that wise man also teach such people to join their palms together and utter, "Namu Amida Butsu," then because they have uttered the Name of that Buddha, they will be released from the sins they committed during five billion kalpas of birth and death. At that very moment, that Buddha will send his own transformation body together with the transformation bodies of the [Bodhisattvas] Avalokiteśvara and Mahāsthāmaprāpta. They will come before the practitioners with words of praise and say,

93

"Good children, because you have uttered the Buddha's Name, all of your sins have been destroyed. So we have come to welcome you."

In the *Commentary* on the same sutra it is said:

One hears the Buddha's transformation body tell only of the merits of uttering the Buddha's Name when he says, "We have come to welcome you." He does not discuss the matter of listening to the sutras. Clearly the intent of the Buddha's Vow is only to encourage one to recite the Name with right mindfulness. The efficiency and speed with which this practice brings about Rebirth cannot be compared with the Miscellaneous Practices performed with a distracted mind. The *Meditation Sutra* and the various Mahayana sutras praise and encourage the recitation of the Name, saying that it will produce benefits of vital importance. This fact should surely be known.

For my part, I wish to say that the good practice of listening to the sutras is not part of the Original Vow. Because it is one of the miscellaneous karmic acts, the Transformation Buddha will not praise it. Because the practice of the Nembutsu is the Right Practice of the Original Vow, the Transformation Buddha will praise it. Moreover, listening to the sutras and uttering the Nembutsu are different in the amount of sin they can extinguish.

In the *Commentary on the Meditation Sutra* it is said:

Someone may ask, "Why does listening to the names of the sutras in the twelve divisions take away the sins of only a thousand kalpas while a single utterance of the Buddha's Name takes away the sins of five million kalpas? Can you explain the meaning of this?" In answer I should say that the person who has committed sin is already burdened with heavy encumbrances. Then, in addition, the death agony comes and closes in on him or her. Hence, even though a good teacher may explain many sutras, the mind that hears and tries to digest them is torn by distractions. Since the mind is distracted, the remission of sins is relatively slight. Although the Buddha's Name is one, it both embraces the distracted mind and settles the heart. Also it can teach one to recite the Name with right mindfulness so that the mind is settled and the sins of many kalpas are taken away.

Chapter XI

The Nembutsu Practice Is Praised above the Miscellaneous Practices

*Passages That Contrast the Nembutsu with the Many
Miscellaneous Practices and Praise It Alone*

The *Meditation Sutra* says: 13c

> It should be clearly understood that he who thinks of the
> Buddha is, among his fellows, like the white lotus flower.
> The [Bodhisattvas] Avalokiteśvara and Mahāsthāmaprāpta
> become his excellent friends. He will surely sit on the seat of
> Enlightenment and be born in the dwelling of all the Buddhas.

In the *Commentary* on the same sutra it is said:

> The passage of the *Meditation Sutra* which begins with "He
> who practices the Nembutsu" and continues up to "be born
> in the dwelling of all the Buddhas" clearly demonstrates
> that the Nembutsu Samādhi possesses supreme meritori-
> ous power and cannot even be compared with the Miscella-
> neous Good Practices. This section has five parts.
>   The first explains the single-minded recitation of the
> Name of Amida. The second explains that the person who
> recites the Name is to be singled out for praise. The third
> explains that the person who continually utters the Nembutsu

is a rare being who is beyond compare and is therefore likened to the white lotus flower. The white lotus flower is called the most excellent flower among men, the rarest flower, the flower of the highest quality among men, and the most wonderfully fine flower among men. Also, it is traditionally known as the "Ts'ai Flower." Thus, whoever recites the Nembutsu is a most excellent, a wondrously good, and a person of the highest level of the superior class and the rarest and most excellent of all people. The fourth explains that anyone who single-mindedly recites the Name of Amida will always be sheltered by the protection of the Bodhisattvas Avalokiteśvara and Mahāsthāmaprāpta. They will be like intimate friends and teachers. The fifth explains that such practitioners will already in their present lives enjoy these benefits. When they lay aside their present lives, they will enter into the dwelling of the Buddhas, the Pure Land. Upon arriving there, they will pass long periods listening to the Dharma and will go about honoring and making offerings to the Buddhas and Bodhisattvas. By thus bringing their practice to perfection, they will fully enjoy its fruits. Why then should one think that the seat of Enlightenment is far away?

Someone might ask the following question, "When the [*Meditation*] *Sutra* says, 'If a person practices the Nembutsu, it should be clearly understood that . . .', it refers only to the practitioner of the Nembutsu and praises him alone. Why then did the commentator say, 'Indeed, this cannot even be compared with the Miscellaneous Good Practices . . .'? And why—as opposed to such Miscellaneous Good Practices—did he praise the Nembutsu alone?"

In answer I say that the meaning is clear even though in the text it is obscure. We know this is true because the [*Meditation*] *Sutra* has already taught us the Contemplative and Distractive Good Practices and the practice of the Nembutsu as well. However, among these practices, only the Nembutsu was singled out and compared with the white lotus flower. Unless it is compared with the Miscellaneous Good Practices, how can the merit of the Nembutsu, which surpasses all the other good practices, be properly revealed? Hence the words, "Whoever recites the Nembutsu is the most excellent [of all people]" praise that person in comparison with evil people. The words "is wondrously good" praise such a one in comparison with coarse and bad people. The words, "a person of the highest level of the superior class" praise such a one in comparison with people of the lowest level of the lower class. The word "rarest" praises such a person in comparison with ordinary people. The words, "most excellent of all people" extol him or her in comparison with the most inferior type of people.

Someone might ask, "If the Nembutsu [practitioner] is designated as being the highest level of the superior class of people, then why is it not explained in the section on the highest level of the superior class, and why is the Nembutsu explained only in the section on the lowest level of the lower class?" In answer I say, "Was it not already said above that the practice of the Nembutsu broadly covers all the nine classes of people?" This was shown in the above-cited passage from *The Collection on Essentials for Rebirth* which said, "In accord with the superiority or inferiority of their capacities, they can be divided into the nine classes." Furthermore, the lowest level of the lower class of people are those who commit such serious acts as the five deadly sins, but the other practices are not capable of remitting and extinguishing these sins. Only the power of the Nembutsu can destroy these kinds of sins. Therefore, it was for the sake of the most wicked and inferior people that the highest Dharma of the supremely good practice was expounded. For example, the root cause of the sickness of ignorance cannot be cured without the treasured medicine called the Middle Way. Now the five deadly sins are the origin of this serious illness, and the Nembutsu is the treasured miraculous medicine. Without this medicine, how could such an illness be cured?

For this reason, Kōbō Daishi, in his *Treatise on the Two Teachings*, quotes the *Sutra of the Six Pāramitās* as follows:

14a

Thirdly, the Dharma treasure is the Right Dharma expounded by the countless Buddhas of the past, which I [Śākyamuni] too now teach. It is the whole collection of the eighty-four thousand kinds of wonderful Dharma teaching. These teachings discipline and bring to maturity sentient beings who are karmically related to them. They cause Ānanda and other great disciples to remember and to hold fast to them even though they are heard but once. They are divided into five groups. The first is the sutras, the second is the *vinaya*, the third is the *abhidharma*, the fourth is the *prajñāpāramitā*, and the fifth is the *dhāraṇī*. I expound each of these five kinds of collections (*piṭaka*s) in order to teach and convert all sentient beings, each in accord with their own karmic propensities.

I shall expound the *piṭaka* of the sutras for those sentient beings who desire to dwell in the mountains and forests, always being in tranquillity in order to practice meditation.

I shall expound the *piṭaka* of the *vinaya* for those sentient beings who study and take delight in proper conduct, who abide by the Right Dharma, and who live harmoniously together in order to preserve the Right Dharma forever.

I shall expound the [*piṭaka* of the] *abhidharma* for those sentient beings who delight in expounding the Right Dharma, distinguishing its substance and its appearances, and who complete the full course of investigation to arrive at its ultimate depths.

I shall expound the *piṭaka* of the *prajñāpāramitā* for those sentient beings who wish to learn the true wisdom of the Mahayana, cutting off the discriminations that arise from attachment to either the self or the dharmas.

There are also those sentient beings who cannot uphold the sutras, the *vinaya* discipline, the *abhidharma*, or the *prajñāpāramitā*. Also, there are those sentient beings who perform all kinds of evil deeds, committing various kinds of

serious sins such as the four grievous deeds, the eight grievous deeds, the five sins that deserve the hell of unceasing
torment, the slander of the Mahayana sutras, the sins of
the *icchantika*s, and the like. It is to enable such people to
destroy these bonds and quickly to achieve emancipation
and sudden realization of nirvana that I expound the *piṭaka*   14b
of the many *dhāraṇī*s.

These five *piṭaka*s can be compared to milk, cream, butter, cheese, and finally the wondrous ghee. The sutras are
like milk. The subjugation [of the passions] is like cream.
The doctrine of the *abhidharma* is like butter. Supreme
wisdom of the Mahayana is like cheese. The *Dhāraṇī* Gateway is like ghee.

The flavor of ghee is sublime and better than the flavors
of milk, cream, butter, and cheese. It takes away all illnesses
and makes sentient beings happy and at peace in mind and
body. The *Dhāraṇī* Gateway is foremost; better than the
study of sutras and the rest. It can take away grievous sins
and liberate all sentient beings from birth and death by
causing them to realize the Dharma body of nirvana's peace
and bliss.

The five sins that deserve the hell of unceasing torment are the
five deadly sins. Without the wonderful medicine of ghee, the sickness of these five sins would be extremely difficult to cure. The
Nembutsu is the same. In the teaching of Rebirth, the Nembutsu
Samādhi is like a *dhāraṇī* or like ghee. Without the medicinal
ghee of the Nembutsu Samādhi, it would be extremely difficult to
cure the sickness of deep and grievous crimes such as the five
deadly sins. One ought surely to realize this.

Someone might ask, "If that is the case, why should the Nembutsu be taught to those of the highest level of the lower class,
who have committed the minor sins of the ten evils?"

I say in answer that if the Nembutsu Samādhi destroys even
grievous sins, how much more will it destroy minor sins! This is

not true of the other practices. Some destroy minor sins but will not destroy serious ones. Others will extinguish only one of these but will not extinguish both of them. This is not so with the Nembutsu. It extinguishes both the minor and the serious and cures everything completely. It is, for example, like the *Agada* medicine, which cures all illnesses of any kind whatever. For this reason, the Nembutsu is the king of Samādhis.

Generally speaking, dividing men and women into the nine classes of people is only a tentative device. Repenting of the five deadly sins [mentioned in the lowest level of the lowest class] also applies to the highest level of the superior class. The marvelous practice of reading and chanting the sutras may also be taken up by those at the rank of the lowest level of the lower class. On the other hand, it is also possible that those who commit the minor sins of the ten evils, such as the breaking of the precepts and other less serious offenses, may find themselves in any of the ranks from the superior to the lower classes.

Further, understanding the most fundamental meaning of the Dharma and awakening the Bodhi mind may also be done by one within any of the ranks from the superior to the lower classes. Thus, any one of the Dharmas is applicable to any of the nine classes. Therefore, speaking in terms of classes, there are, in all, nine times nine, or eighty-one classes. Nor is this all, as Chia-ts'ai pointed out, "Sentient beings' practices are of a thousand varieties. And so, when they are reborn in the Pure Land, there are ten thousand variations in their perception of that Land." Hence do not become quickly attached to a certain interpretation after only briefly glancing at the text. Among these practices, the Nembutsu is the best. That is why the analogy of the lotus flower is used. One should take care to understand properly the meaning of this analogy.

Moreover the Bodhisattvas Avalokiteśvara and Mahāsthāma-prāpta like a shadow following an object, will never separate themselves from the Nembutsu practitioner even for an instant. This is not true of other practices. Further, the Nembutsu practitioners, after they have laid aside their present life, will certainly be reborn in the Land of Supreme Bliss. It is uncertain [whether or not people who perform the other practices] will be reborn.

Generally speaking, [the Nembutsu practitioner] is extolled   14c
by the five kinds of esteem and praise and is blessed with the close protection of the two honored ones. These are the present benefits. The future benefit is that [the practitioner] will be reborn in the Pure Land and eventually become a Buddha.

Furthermore, the Dhyāna Master Tao-ch'o has declared two benefits, initial and final, for the one practice of the Nembutsu. He says in the *Collection of Passages on the Land of Peace and Bliss*:

> Sentient beings who practice the Nembutsu are embraced by Amida and never abandoned; at the end of their lives they will certainly be reborn in the Pure Land. This is called the initial benefit. The final benefit, according to the *Sutra of Avalokiteśvara's Prediction*, is as follows. Amida Buddha will live in the world for an immense period of time, for long kalpas containing billions of years, and then he will pass into nirvana. At the time of this complete nirvana, only the Bodhisattvas Avalokiteśvara and Mahāshtāmaprāpta will remain in the Land of Peace and Bliss, guiding [the beings] of all the ten directions. The period after the Buddha's nirvana is exactly like that when he dwells in the world. However, not all of the sentient beings who live in the Pure Land during this period of nirvana will be able to see the Buddha. Only those who have wholeheartedly and single-mindedly concentrated on Amida Buddha and so have been reborn in the Pure Land will see Amida as always present before them and not as having disappeared into nirvana. This is the final benefit.

One certainly should be aware of this fact. The Nembutsu offers these two benefits, the initial and the final, as has been shown above, in either the present or in future lives. This should surely be known.

Chapter XII

Only the Nembutsu Was Transmitted to Ānanda

*Passages Relating That Śākyamuni Did Not Entrust
to Ānanda the Various Contemplative and Distractive
Practices but Entrusted to Him the Nembutsu Alone*

The *Meditation Sutra* says, "The Buddha said to Ānanda, 'You
must hold fast to these words! To hold fast to them is to hold fast
to the Name of the Buddha of Immeasurable Life.'" The *Commentary* on the same sutra says:

> The passage, "The Buddha said to Ānanda, 'You must hold
> fast to these words!'" and so forth, correctly explains that
> Śākyamuni transmitted Amida's Name to Ānanda so that
> it would endure far into future ages. It is true that the
> benefits of the Two Gateways known as the Contemplative
> and Distractive Practices had been expounded in a previous section of the sutra. Nevertheless, when seen in terms
> of the meaning of the Buddha's Original Vow, it is actually
> to have sentient beings wholeheartedly and single-mindedly
> utter the Name of Amida Buddha.

In my opinion, when one ponders the above words of the *Commentary*, one sees that there are two kinds of practice: one, the Contemplative and Distractive Practices, and the other, the Nembutsu.

First, we shall consider the Contemplative and Distractive Practices and treat them separately: first the Contemplative Good Practices and next the Distractive Good Practices.

A. The Contemplative Good Practices

The Contemplative Good Practices are thirteen in number: (1) to contemplate the sun, (2) to contemplate water, (3) to envision the ground [of the Pure Land], (4) to envision its jewel trees, (5) to envision its jewel ponds, (6) to envision its jewel towers, (7) to envision its lotus blossom thrones, (8) to contemplate holy images, (9) to envision Amida Buddha, (10) to envision Avalokiteśvara, (11) to envision Mahāsthāmaprāpta, (12) to envision general aspects of one's own Rebirth, and (13) to envision the various objects [of the Pure Land]. These are explained in detail in the sutra. Even though other practices are lacking, if anyone performs one or several of these according to his own capacity, then he will be able to attain Rebirth. An explanation to this effect appears in that sutra. Therefore, do not doubt or question it.

15a

B. The Distractive Good Practices

Next, there are two kinds of Distractive Good Practices. One is the three meritorious practices, and the other, is the practices for the nine classes of people.

First, regarding the three meritorious practices, the [*Meditation*] *Sutra* says:

> The first of these is filial duty toward one's father and mother, reverence for one's teachers and elders, a compassionate heart that avoids any kind of killing, and performance of the ten good practices. The second is to hold fast to the Three Refuges, to observe the various precepts, and not to violate the rules of proper conduct. The third is to awaken the Bodhi mind, to have deep faith in the law of [karmic] causality, to read and recite the Mahayana sutras, and to encourage other practitioners.

There are two kinds of "filial duty toward one's father and mother": one is a worldly filial duty and the other is a transcendent filial duty. Worldly filial duty is as described in the *Book of Filial Piety* and elsewhere. Filial duty that transcends this world is as described in the Vinaya, which speaks of the prescribed method of serving the parents responsible for one's birth.

There are also two kinds of "reverence for one's teachers and elders": one is reverence for one's worldly teachers and elders, the other is reverence for one's teachers and elders in matters that transcend this world. Worldly masters teach benevolence, righteousness, courtesy, wisdom, trustworthiness, and the like. Masters in matters that transcend this world teach the Two Gateways of the Holy Path and the Pure Land and the like. Even though other practices are lacking, filial piety and reverence for one's parents and teachers can be the karmic act for Rebirth in the Pure Land.

There are also two interpretations of the phrase, "the compassionate heart that avoids any kind of killing and performance of the ten good deeds." According to the first interpretation, "the compassionate heart that avoids any kind of killing" is the first of the four boundless minds, namely boundless love. The other three are understood as being included in the first. Even though other practices are lacking, [the presence of] these four boundless minds can be the karma by which one is reborn in the Pure Land.

Next, concerning the "performance of the ten good practices": (1) not to kill, (2) not to steal, (3) not to commit adultery, (4) not to lie, (5) not to speak in an irresponsible and flamboyant manner, (6) not to use abusive language, (7) not to utter words that cause enmity between two or more persons, (8) not to covet, (9) to avoid anger, and (10) not to hold heretical views.

According to the second interpretation the two phrases, "the loving heart that avoids any kind of killing," and "performance of the ten good practices," are combined into one phrase. "The loving heart that avoids any kind of killing," is not the first of the four boundless minds, namely boundless love, but the first of the ten good deeds, namely "not to kill." Hence we should know that [the first phrase] corresponds precisely to one of the ten good deeds.

Even though all other practices are lacking, the performance of the ten good practices can be the karma by which one is reborn.

"To hold fast to the Three Refuges" is to take refuge in the Buddha, the Dharma, and the Sangha. There are two [interpretations] of this. The first understands this as referring to the Three Treasures [as explained in] the Mahayana; the second, to the Three Treasures [as explained in] the Hinayana.

There are also two interpretations of "to observe the various precepts." One understands it to refer to the precepts of the Mahayana; the other, to the Hinayana precepts.

"Not to violate the rules of proper conduct," also has two interpretations, one being the so-called eighty thousand rules of the Mahayana and the other, the so-called three thousand rules of the Hinayana.

Concerning the meaning of "awaken the Bodhi mind," the masters' opinions are divided. The Tendai school speaks of the Bodhi mind in the "Four Teachings," namely the Piṭaka Teaching, the Common Teaching, the Particular Teaching, and the Perfect Teaching. These are treated in some detail in the text *Meditation and* 15b *Contemplation*.

In the Shingon school, three kinds of Bodhi mind are distinguished: that of making vows and performing practices, that of contemplating the supreme principle, and that of attaining realization in *samādhi*. These are treated fully in the *Treatise on the Bodhi Mind*.

The Kegon school also has its concept of the Bodhi mind. It is explained in the *Meaning of the Bodhi Mind*, in the *Way of the Mind Serenely Strolling in the Land of Peace and Bliss*, and in other works.

Both the Sanron and the Hossō schools also have their notion of the Bodhi mind. It is explained in detail in their commentaries and other treatises. Further, Shan-tao also interprets the meaning of the Bodhi mind. He speaks at length about it in his *Commentary*. Although the phrase "awaken the Bodhi mind" remains the same, its meaning differs according to each school.

In this way, it is clear that the one phrase, "Bodhi mind," is widely discussed in the many sutras, both the exoteric and the esoteric ones. Its meaning is vast and profound, and its implications are immeasurably deep. I pray that the many Buddhist practitioners will avoid fixing on only one meaning and shutting out the many others. Everyone among those who seek Rebirth in the Pure Land should strive diligently to awaken the Bodhi mind in the manner proper to their own school. Even though all the other practices are lacking, awakening the Bodhi mind can be the karmic action for Rebirth in the Pure Land.

Regarding "deep faith in [karmic] causality," there are two kinds: one is [faith in] the law of worldly cause and effect and the other is faith in cause and effect that transcend this world. Worldly cause and effect is that of the six paths, as is explained in the *Sutra of Correct Dharma Thought*. Cause and effect that transcend the world are karmic causes and effects relevant to the four grades of Holy People, as explained in the sutras of both the Mahayana and the Hinayana. If we classify all of the sutras in terms of these two kinds of cause and effect, we get different views, according to the different schools of thought.

According to the understanding of the Tendai, the *Avataṃsaka Sutra* teaches two types of cause and effect: that of the Buddha and that of the Bodhisattva. The *Āgama*s also expound two kinds of cause and effect, namely that of the *Śrāvaka* and that of the *Pratyekabuddha*. The various *Vaipulya* sutras expound the causes and effects of the Four Vehicles, the various *Prajñāpāramitā* sutras teach common, particular, and perfect types of cause and effect, the *Lotus Sutra* teaches the causes required for becoming a Buddha and the effects of Buddhahood, and the *Nirvana Sutra* also expounds the causes and effects of the Four Vehicles.

In this manner the phrase "deep faith in cause and effect" pervades all the teachings of the Buddha throughout his whole life. For all those who seek Rebirth in the Pure Land, even though they fail to perform any other practice, deep faith in cause and effect can become a karmic action for Rebirth.

"Reading and chanting the Mahayana sutras" is divided into two parts: "reading and chanting" and "the Mahayana sutras." The former, by mentioning only two of the five kinds of Dharma Masters—namely those who read the sutras and those who recite them—actually refers to the other three as well, namely "those who uphold the sutras," and so on. In terms of the ten kinds of Dharma practice, "reading and reciting the sutras" refers to the other eight kinds as well, namely "copying the sutras," "reverencing the sutras," and so on.

"Mahayana" stands in contrast to "Hinayana." It does not refer to any one sutra in particular but rather to all the Mahayana sutras in general. According to the Buddha's intent "all" refers to all the Mahayana sutras that the Buddha expounded during his whole life. Among these sutras expounded during his whole life, there are those that were compiled and those not compiled. Among those already compiled, some are still hidden in the dragon palace and are not yet disseminated among men; others are still remaining in India and have not yet arrived in China.

Now with regards to those sutras that have already been brought over and translated, the *Chen-yüan Catalogue of Scriptures Contained in the Piṭaka*, compiled in the T'ang Dynasty contains a total of 637 texts of Mahayana sutras, both exoteric and esoteric, in 2883 fascicles. They begin with the *Larger Prajñā-pāramitā Sutra* of 600 fascicles and end with the *Sutra of the Dharma's Eternal Dwelling*. All these should certainly be understood as included in the one phrase: "reading and reciting the Mahayana sutras."

The practitioners hoping for the Western Paradise may—each in accord with his own preference—read and recite either the *Lotus Sutra* or the *Avataṃsaka Sutra* and turn it into a karmic action for Rebirth. Or else these practitioners may uphold, read, and recite the *Vairocana Sutra*, the *King of the Teaching*, or the various rites dedicated to the Holy Ones, and turn this into karmic action for Rebirth. Or else they may explain and copy the *Prajñā*, the *Vaipulya*, the *Nirvana*, and the other sutras and turn this into karmic action for Rebirth. This is the intention of the *Meditation Sutra* in the Pure Land School.

It may be asked, "The basic principles of the Exoteric and the Esoteric Teachings differ. Why then do you include the Esoteric in the Exoteric?" My reply is that the above exposition does not lump together the basic principles of the Esoteric and Exoteric. It simply points out that the scriptures of both are joined together as Mahayana sutras in the *Chen-yüan Catalogue of Scriptures Contained in the Piṭaka*. For this reason, they are both included in the one phrase, "reading and reciting the Mahayana sutras."

It may further be asked, "Why do you include the *Lotus Sutra* in the sutras the Buddha taught prior to the *Lotus Sutra*?" My answer is that I do not use the word "include" to discriminate between Provisional and Real, Partial and Perfect Teachings, and so forth. The words "reading and reciting the Mahayana sutras" cover all the Mahayana sutras, both those which came before and those which came after. Those "before" refer to the Mahayana sutras which came before the *Meditation Sutra;* "after" refers to those which followed the proclamation of that sutra at the king's palace.

Reference was made simply to "the Mahayana sutras." No distinction was intended between Provisional and Real Teachings. That being the case, the phrase correctly applies equally to such Mahayana sutras as the *Avataṃsaka* and *Vaipulya*, as well as to those like the *Prajñā*, the *Lotus*, and the *Nirvana*.

The words, "encourages others to perform these practices" mean that one should encourage people to perform both the various Contemplative and Distractive Good Practices as well as the practice of the Nembutsu Samādhi.

Next we treat of the nine classes of people. The three meritorious practices, which were explained earlier, are expanded into the practices for the nine classes of aspirants.

The "loving heart that avoids any kind of killing" mentioned in the section on the "highest level of the superior class," corresponds to the third phrase in the above-quoted "worldly meritorious practices."

The next phrase, "practice of observing the various precepts" corresponds exactly to the second phrase of the second meritorious practice described above: "to observe the various precepts." The next, "reading and reciting the Mahayana sutras" corresponds to the third phrase of the above-described third meritorious practice: "reading and reciting the Mahayana sutras." The next, "the practice of the six concentrations" has the same meaning as the above-cited third phrase in the third meritorious practice.

16a "To understand well the ultimate meaning," mentioned in the section on "the middle level of the superior class," corresponds to the meaning of the second and third parts of the third meritorious practice explained earlier. "To have deep faith in karmic cause and effect, and to awaken the Bodhi mind," mentioned in the "lowest level of the superior class," corresponds to the first and second phrases of the third meritorious practice above.

"Accepting and observing the Five Precepts," mentioned in the "highest level of the middle class," corresponds to the meaning of the second phrase of the second meritorious practice above. "To uphold for one day and one night the eight regulating precepts," mentioned in the "middle level of the middle class," corresponds to the second meritorious practices above. "Filial duty to father and mother, and practicing worldly benevolence and compassion," mentioned in the "lowest level of the middle class," corresponds to the meaning of the first and second phrases in the first meritorious practice above.

The highest level of the lower class is composed of sinful people who commit the ten evils. If at the end of their lives they utter but one Nembutsu, their sins will be destroyed and they will attain Rebirth. The middle level of the lower class is made up of sinful people who break the precepts. If at the end of their lives they hear of the merits of the Buddha and his Land, their sins will be destroyed and they will attain Rebirth. The lowest level of the lower class is made up of the people who commit the five deadly sins. If at the end of their lives they utter the Nembutsu ten times, their sins will be destroyed and they will attain Rebirth.

Even though the people belonging to these last three classes do nothing but evil deeds in their ordinary lives and do not desire Rebirth, nevertheless, at the end of their lives they may chance to meet a good teacher for the first time and thereby obtain Rebirth. If one wishes to draw a parallel between these and the three meritorious practices described above, [these practices of the three lower classes] correspond to the third of the meritorious practices: "[reading and chanting] the Mahayana sutras."

The above is only a rough summary of the Contemplative and Distractive Good Practices. This is the implication of the *Commentary on the Meditation Sutra* when it says, "The benefits of the Two Gateways known as the Contemplative and Distractive Good Practices have already been expounded previously . . ."

C. The Nembutsu Practice

Next we treat the Nembutsu: the wholehearted utterance of the Name of Amida Buddha. The meaning of the Nembutsu is as it is usually given. Now the passage says, "correctly explains that Śākyamuni transmitted Amida's Name to Ānanda so that it would endure far into the future ages." Although [Śākyamuni] had in that sutra already expounded at length the various Contemplative and Distractive Good Practices; nevertheless, he did not transmit these Contemplative and Distractive Practices to Ānanda for transmission to succeeding ages. Only the single practice of the Nembutsu Samādhi was entrusted to Ānanda for transmission into the far distant future.

One might ask why the various Contemplative and Distractive Practices were not entrusted to Ānanda for transmission [and pursue the following line of reasoning]: [Even if you argue that Śākyamuni] did not transmit them because he disliked the fact that they include a mixture of shallow and deep karmic activities, [you must nevertheless admit that] the three meritorious practices include both shallowness and depth. Filial duty to one's father and mother, as well as reverence for one's teachers and elders, are shallow practices, while observing the various precepts, awakening the Bodhi mind, deep faith in karmic cause and effect, and reading and chanting the Mahayana sutras are deep practices. [Logically then] the shallow practices should have been discarded; but the deep practices would have been entrusted [to Ānanda]. If [you argue that] the distinction was made between shallowness and depth of meditation, and that the shallow kinds of meditation were rejected, [still you will have to admit that] the thirteen types of contemplation include both shallow and deep [practices]. To contemplate the sun and water is shallow contemplation, but the following eleven—from envisioning the ground to envisioning the various splendors of the Pure Land—are deep [modes of] contemplation. The shallow contemplation should have been discarded, and the deep contemplation should have been transmitted [to Ānanda]. Further, among the eleven, the ninth concentration is to envision Amida Buddha. This is the Samādhi of Seeing the Buddha. [Śākyamuni may possibly] have cast aside the other twelve and could have transmitted to Ānanda only the Samādhi of Seeing the Buddha. Furthermore, the "Section on Profound Meanings" in the *Commentary* on the same [*Meditation Sutra*] says, "This sutra has as its essence both the Samādhi of Seeing the Buddha and the Nembutsu Samādhi." These two practices form the essence of this sutra. Why then would Śākyamuni discard the Samādhi of Seeing the Buddha and transmit to Ānanda only the Nembutsu Samādhi?

16b

[To such a mode of reasoning] I answer that [the *Commentary* says], "When seen in terms of the meaning of the Buddha's Original Vow, actually it is to have sentient beings single-mindedly and wholeheartedly utter the Name of Amida Buddha." The various Contemplative and Distractive Practices are not [the intent of] the Original Vow. That is why they were not transmitted [to Ānanda]. Further, even though the Samādhi of Seeing the Buddha is the most outstanding among these practices, still it is not [the intent of] the Original Vow. That is why it was not transmitted to Ānanda. The Nembutsu Samādhi is [the intent of] the Buddha's Original Vow. That is why he transmitted it.

The above-cited words of the *Commentary*, "When seen in terms of the meaning of the Buddha's Original Vow" refer to the Eighteenth of the Forty-eight Vows in the *Two-Volume [Larger] Sutra*. "Single-mindedly and wholeheartedly to utter" refers to "single-minded and wholehearted meditation on" found in the part of the three classes of people in this same sutra. The meaning of the Original Vow has already been explained in detail above.

It may be asked, "If such is the case, then why did Śākyamuni not expound in a straightforward manner the Nembutsu practice of the Original Vow instead of going to the trouble of explaining the various Contemplative and Distractive Good Practices, which are not included in the Original Vow?"

I answer that the Nembutsu practice of the Original Vow has already been expounded in detail in the *Two-Volume Sutra*. Hence it is not explained here again. Furthermore, Śākyamuni expounded the Contemplative and Distractive Good Practices in order to reveal the superiority of the Nembutsu over the other practices. Without the Contemplative and Distractive Practices, how could he have made clear the special preeminence of the Nembutsu?

This is for example, like the preeminence of the Lotus Teaching among the three teachings. If the doctrine of the three teachings did not exist, how could it be made clear that the Lotus Teaching is best? Therefore, the Contemplative and Distractive Practices were expounded only in order that they might be abandoned, while the Nembutsu Samādhi was expounded so that it could be established. Still, the various Contemplative and Distractive Good Practices are all difficult to evaluate. In general, the Contemplative Good Practices involve seeing Amida Buddha and his Land as clearly as looking at an image in a mirror. [With these] the desire for Rebirth will arise as quickly as pointing to the palm of one's hand. The power of one contemplation removes the sins and faults of many kalpas. The merits of all these [thirteen] contemplations can eventually bring the marvelous reward of Samādhi. Thus the man who desires Rebirth should practice the contemplations. Among these the ninth, in which one visualizes Amida's actual body, is the method for [achieving] the Samādhi of

Seeing the Buddha. If one brings this practice to fruition, one will actually see the body of Amida. Then, because one sees Amida's body, one will actually be able to see all the Buddhas. Because one sees all the Buddhas, one receives the promise of assured Enlightenment in front of the Buddhas. The benefits of this contemplation are extremely profound.

However, in the section on "dissemination" of the *Meditation Sutra* the Tathāgata Śākyamuni gave Ānanda a special command, entrusting to him the task of spreading everywhere the Dharma concerning the practice necessary for Rebirth in the Pure Land. He did not favor the method of envisioning the Buddha and did not entrust it to Ānanda, but he chose the method of the Nembutsu and did entrust that to him. He did not entrust to him even the method of the Samādhi of Seeing the Buddha, much less that of contemplating the sun, water, and the other objects. Hence, the thirteen contemplations are not practices transmitted to Ānanda. Thus if people in this world wish to perform the practice of seeing the Buddha and do not practice the Nembutsu, they are not only going against Amida's Original Vow made in the distant past, they are also at variance with the intention of Śākyamuni when he entrusted [the Nembutsu] to Ānanda in the recent past. Practitioners should carefully consider this.

Next, among the Distractive Good Practices there are both observing the precepts of the Mahayana and observing those of the Hinayana. People in the world regard the practice of observing the precepts as essential for entering into the truth. They believe that those who break the precepts cannot be reborn in the Pure Land.

There is also the practice of awakening the Bodhi mind. People regard the Bodhi mind as an essential point for [Rebirth in the] Pure Land. They believe that those who have not awakened the Bodhi mind cannot attain Rebirth.

There is also the practice of understanding the highest truth, which is insight into the essential principle. People also consider this principle to be the wellspring of Buddhahood. One cannot seek

16c

the Buddha's Land without this principle and those who lack it cannot be reborn.

Further, there is the practice of reading and chanting the Mahayana sutras. All people think that by reading and chanting the Mahayana sutras it is possible to be reborn in the Pure Land, and that those who do not read and chant the Mahayana sutras cannot be reborn. There are two modes of this practice: one is chanting the sutras and the other is chanting the *dhāraṇī*s. The first refers to chanting the *Prajñā*, the *Lotus*, and other Mahayana sutras. The other practice refers to chanting the "Wish-Fulfilling," the "Most August," the "Brightly Shining," the "Amida," and other sacred *dhāraṇī*s.

Generally speaking, one should revere all the eleven types of the Distractive Good Practices. However, the four practices just mentioned are especially appreciated by people of the present age. They have almost suppressed the practice of the Nembutsu.   17a

If one carefully ponders the intent of the [*Meditation*] sutra, however, one will see that it is not these various practices that were entrusted to Ānanda for future transmission. Only the one Nembutsu practice was so entrusted for the ages that would follow. One ought surely to know that the reason why Śākyamuni did not entrust these various practices to Ānanda was that they are completely absent from Amida's Original Vow. The reason why Śākyamuni transmitted the Nembutsu to him was that it is in accord with Amida's Original Vow.

Furthermore, the reason why Master Shan-tao abandoned the manifold practices and took refuge in the Nembutsu was that it was unquestionably in accord with Amida's Original Vow, and that Śākyamuni did transmit these practices to Ānanda. One should realize that it is for these reasons that the manifold practices are not in accord with either the capacities of the people or the nature of the present age. It is Rebirth through the Nembutsu that corresponds with people's capacities and with the times. How could both the people's striving and the Buddha's response thereto come to naught?

One ought clearly to understand that Śākyamuni first opened the Gateway of the Contemplative and Distractive Good Practices in response to the wishes of other people. He later closed this gateway in accordance with his own wish. The only gateway which, once opened, will remain unclosed for long aeons is that of the Nembutsu. Practitioners should know this is the intent of Amida's Original Vow and of Śākyamuni's act of entrusting it [to Ānanda].

Also, the words "future ages," according to the implication of the *Two-Volume Sutra*, refer to the hundred-year period following the distant end of the ten thousand-year Age of the Dharma's Decadence. The phrase "far into the future" includes recent time. For if this teaching is good for the period following the complete extinction of the Dharma, then it is even more appropriate for the Age of the Decadence of the Dharma. And if it holds true for that age, then how much more so for the previous Ages of the Right Dharma and the Semblance of the Dharma!

Accordingly one should understand that the Way of Rebirth through the Nembutsu is possible for the three Ages of the Right Dharma, the Semblance [of the Dharma], and the Degeneration of the Dharma as well as the hundred-year period after its complete extinction.

Chapter XIII

The Nembutsu Is the Source
of Much Good

*Passages Attesting That the Nembutsu Gives Rise to
Much Virtue While the Miscellaneous Good Practices
Give Rise to But Little*

The *Amida Sutra* says:

> It is impossible to be reborn in that Land by means of little
> goodness and virtue. O Śāriputra, if a good man or woman
> hears an exposition about Amida Buddha and with his or
> her whole heart takes firm and undistracted hold on his
> Name for one day, for two days, or for three, four, five, six,
> or seven days, then at the time when life is about to end,
> Amida Buddha together with the assembly of the many Holy
> Ones will be present before his or her very eyes. Such a
> person, with mind unperturbed at the time of death, will
> attain Rebirth in Amida Buddha's Land of Supreme Bliss.

Shan-tao, interpreting this passage, says:

> Because [the Land of] Supreme Bliss is the world of uncon-
> ditioned nirvana, it is difficult to be reborn there by means
> of the Miscellaneous Good Practices that correspond to
> people's varying capacities. That is why the Tathāgata chose
> the needed Dharma and taught that one should think solely
> and wholeheartedly on Amida Buddha. One should do this

119

17b

for seven days and seven nights with no break in attention. When undertaking longer periods of practice, one should do this even more. Just as their lives are about to end, a multitude of Holy Beings bearing lotus pedestals with them will appear to such people. With their bodies and minds exulting, they will be seated on these golden lotus pedestals, and when thus seated, they will immediately gain insight into the unproduced [quality of all things]. In an instant, they will be welcomed and be led before the Buddha himself. Then the Dharma's friends will vie with one another to clothe them in Dharma robes. At that time they will realize the Stage of Non-Retrogression and enter into the Stage of the Three Wisdoms.

In my opinion, the phrase, "It is impossible to be reborn in that Land by means of little goodness and virtue," means that it is difficult to be reborn in that Land through all the other Miscellaneous Practices. For that reason [Shan-tao says], "It is difficult to be reborn there by means of the Miscellaneous Good Practices that correspond to people's varying capacities." The phrase "little goodness" is in contrast with the notion of "much goodness." Thus the Miscellaneous Good Practices are the roots of little goodness, while the Nembutsu is the root of much goodness. This is why the *Passages Concerning the Pure Land* of Lung-shu says:

> The ideographs of the *Amida Sutra* carved in stone in the city of Hsiang-yang—written by Ch'en Jen-leng in the Sui Dynasty—were graceful, and many people prized and enjoyed them. [In this version of the sutra one finds]—after the words "single-mindedly and without distraction"—the following passage of twenty-one ideographs that are left out of the text handed down to us today, "By wholeheartedly holding fast to uttering the Name, one's sins are extinguished. This is the karmic result of much goodness and virtue."

Here one can see that the meaning is not just one of "much" versus "little." There is also the meaning of "great" versus "small": that is to say, the Miscellaneous Good Practices represent small goodness, while the Nembutsu represents great goodness. There is also the connotation of "superior" versus "inferior": the Miscellaneous Good Practices are an inferior [form of] goodness, while the Nembutsu is a superior [form of] goodness. One should understand these meanings.

Chapter XIV

The Many Buddhas Bear Witness Only to the Nembutsu

Passages Attesting That the Many Buddhas of the Six Directions as Numerous as the Sands of the Ganges Do Not Bear Witness to the Other Practices But Only to the Nembutsu

Shan-tao's *Dharma Gate of Contemplation* states:

> Further, as it is said in the *Amida Sutra,* the many Buddhas from the six directions, as numerous as the sands of the Ganges, all stretch forth their tongues throughout the three thousand-fold worlds and earnestly proclaim these words, "While the Buddha yet remains in the world and after his disappearance, all ordinary sinful men who merely turn their attention to and think of Amida Buddha and desire to be reborn in his Pure Land will attain Rebirth. Whether they do this for as long as a hundred years or as little as seven days—or for one day, or [while they utter Amida's Name] ten times, or even once—when they come to die, the Buddha and the assembly of his Holy Ones will come personally to welcome them, and they will attain Rebirth."

> The above Buddhas of the six directions, stretching forth their tongues, have certainly borne witness for such ordinary men. Their sins being extinguished, they will attain Rebirth. If in spite of such witness they fail to attain Rebirth,

then the tongues of the Buddhas in each of the six directions will never return to their mouths once they are extended, but will naturally decay and rot.

Likewise, in the *Hymns in Praise of Rebirth* the same author quotes
the *Amida Sutra* as follows:

> All the Buddhas in the east as numerous as the sands of
> the Ganges and all the Buddhas in the south, west, and
> north, as countless as the sands of the Ganges, as well as in
> the quarters that are above and below, each in their own
> Lands stretch forth their tongues throughout the great three
> thousand-fold worlds and speak words of truth: "You sen-
> tient beings surely ought all to believe in this sutra pro-
> tected by all the Buddhas." Why do we say "protected"? It
> is because they have all given witness to the fact that if any
> sentient being utters the Name of Amida Buddha for one to
> seven days, or even ten times, or at least once, or if one
> should think [of Amida] only a single time, then he will
> certainly attain Rebirth. Because they bear witness to this,
> it is called "the sutra that protects the Nembutsu."

17c

The same text also says:

> The Tathāgatas in each of the six directions stretch forth
> their tongues to bear witness to the fact that anyone who
> wholeheartedly utters Amida's Name will reach the West-
> ern Quarter. Once they arrive there, the lotus flowers will
> open, and they will hear the wonderful Dharma. Then, the
> Vow and practices of the [final] ten stages [of the Bodhi-
> sattva] will spontaneously manifest themselves.

The same author, in his *Commentary on the Meditation Sutra*,
quotes the *Amida Sutra* as follows:

> Further, the Buddhas of all the ten directions, fearing that
> sentient beings would not believe that which the single Bud-
> dha Śākyamuni taught, stretch forth their tongues at the
> same time with a single mind and heart, covering the great

three thousand-fold worlds, and proclaim the words of truth, saying, "You sentient beings ought all to believe what Śākyamuni proclaimed, praised, and bore witness to. That is, if all ordinary men, regardless of whether their sins or goodness be great or small, whether the length of their practice be long or short, all single-mindedly and wholeheartedly utter the Name, at most for a hundred years or at least for one to seven days, then there is no doubt that they will certainly attain Rebirth."

The same author states in his *Liturgical Hymns*:

Practice the Nembutsu without interruption and without any doubt. The Tathāgatas throughout the six directions bear witness that this is not false. If without any distractions one devotes oneself to this practice wholeheartedly with body, speech, and mind, the lotus flower of a hundred treasures will in due time appear.

The Dhyāna Master Fa-chao states in his *Five-Tone Ceremonial Hymns* [*Aspiring for Rebirth in the Pure Land*]:

Among the ten thousand differing practices, it is the most urgent and effective. There is none that surpasses the Gateway of the Pure Land. This was not only proclaimed by the original Master with the golden mouth; it was also handed down and verified at one time by all the Buddhas of the ten directions.

Someone might ask me, "Why did the many Buddhas of the six directions bear witness only to the single practice of the Nembutsu alone?" I answer that according to the understanding of Shan-tao, this is because the Nembutsu is [promised in] the Original Vow of Amida. It is for this reason that they bear witness to it. This is not so with the other practices. Hence, they were not [so confirmed].

It may further be asked, "If the Nembutsu is confirmed because of the Original Vow, then why is it that when the Nembutsu was taught by Śākyamuni in the *Two-Volume Sutra* and the *Meditation*

Sutra [the many Buddhas] did not bear witness to it?" I answer that there are two explanations for this. One is that although the Nembutsu of the Original Vow is taught in the *Two-Volume Sutra* and the *Meditation Sutra*, other practices were also revealed at the same time. That is why no special confirmation was given [to any of them]. But in the [*Amida*] *Sutra*, the Nembutsu alone was expounded, and therefore [the Buddhas] bore witness to it.

18a   The second explanation is that although there are no words of witness for the Nembutsu in the *Two-Volume Sutra*, this witness was already given in the *Amida Sutra*. Using this as an example, we can surely conclude that the Nembutsu expounded in them is also witnessed. The [witnessing] passage is found [only] in this one sutra, but its meaning pervades the other sutras as well. That is why it is said in T'ien-tai's *Treatise on the Ten Doubts:*

> Also the *Amida Sutra*, the *Larger Sutra of Immeasurable Life*, the *Sutra on the Dhāraṇī of the Drum's Sound*, and others state that when Śākyamuni Buddha proclaimed these sutras, all the Buddhas in the worlds of the ten directions, as numerous as the sands of the Ganges, stretched forth their tongues throughout the great three thousand-fold worlds and bore witness to the fact that every sentient being who thinks on Amida Buddha will, because of the Buddha's Original Vow, be borne by the power of this Vow's compassion and will most certainly attain Rebirth in the World of Supreme Bliss.

Chapter XV

All the Buddhas Protect
Those Who Utter the Nembutsu

*Passages Relating How All the Buddhas of the Six
Directions Protect and Remember the Nembutsu Practitioner*

The *Dharma Gate of Contemplation* says:

> Further, as is taught in the *Amida Sutra*, if a man or woman
> single-mindedly and wholeheartedly meditates on Amida
> Buddha and desires Rebirth for a period of from seven days
> and nights up to their whole lifespan, then all the Buddhas
> of the six directions, as many as the sands of the Ganges,
> together will come and always protect him or her. This is
> why that sutra is known as the "sutra of protection." "Pro-
> tection" means that all devils and evil spirits are prevented
> from coming into contact with the practitioner, and also that
> no sudden and calamitous illness, death, or disaster will
> befall him or her; that all misfortunes and obstacles will
> spontaneously disappear. Those whose practice is not whole-
> hearted are excepted.

In the *Hymns in Praise of Rebirth* it is said:

> If anyone calls on the Buddha in hope of Rebirth, he will al-
> ways be protected by all of the Buddhas of the six directions

as numerous as the sands of the Ganges. That is why it is called the "sutra of protection." Since this supreme Vow exists, you should rely on it. Why then do not all the Buddha's children apply themselves [to this practice]?

Someone might ask whether or not it is true that only Tathāgatas of the six directions protect the practitioner. I answer that it is not just the Tathāgatas of the six directions, but also Amida, Avalokiteśvara, and others come and protect them. That is why the *Hymns in Praise of Rebirth* says:

> It is stated in the *Sutra of Ten Rebirths* that if there be sentient beings who think of Amida Buddha and desire Rebirth, then Amida will dispatch twenty-five Bodhisattvas to protect these practitioners. Whether they be walking, sitting, standing still, or lying down, whether in the day or night, at whatever time or in whatever place, devils and evil spirits will be kept from coming into contact with them.

And again, it is said in the *Meditation Sutra* that if anyone extols, reverences, and thinks of Amida Buddha and desires to be reborn in his Land, then that Buddha will send an innumerable host of Transformation Buddhas and Avalokiteśvara and Mahāsthāmaprāpta in countless transformation bodies to protect such a practitioner. Further, together with the above-mentioned twenty-five Bodhisattvas, they will surround him in hundreds and thousands of rows, whether he be walking, standing still, sitting, or lying down, at all times and in every place, day or night, and they will never leave him. Since this supreme benefit is available, one ought surely to rely on it. It is my fervent hope that each one of the many practitioners will seek Rebirth with a sincere heart.

Further, the *Dharma Gate of Contemplation* states:

> Again, as the latter section of the *Meditation Sutra* says, "If a person always meditates with a sincere heart on Amida or on the two Bodhisattvas Avalokiteśvara and Mahāsthāmaprāpta, they will become his excellent friends and

18b

teachers and will, as his guardians, follow him as closely as his own shadow."

The same text further says:

Further, as is taught in the section on practice of the *Sutra of the Samādhi Wherein All the Buddhas Are Present*, "The Buddha declared that if anyone wholeheartedly practices the Samādhi of Meditating on Amida Buddha, then all of the many heavenly beings, including the great guardian kings of the four directions and the eight kinds of guardians of Buddhism such as dragons and *devas*, will, as his protectors, always follow him as closely as his own shadow and joyfully watch over him. Neither devils nor evil spirits nor misfortunes and obstacles nor disasters will come unexpectedly to confuse him." A detailed explanation of this is given in the section on protection and safekeeping [of the same sutra].

It continues:

Those who—except when they enter the place where they practice Samādhi—persevere until the end of their lives in calling Amida Buddha to mind ten thousand times every day will enjoy his protection and have all their sinful obstructions removed. They will further benefit from the fact that the Buddha and the hosts of his holy attendants will always come and protect them. Having been able to enjoy this protection, the span of their lives will be lengthened.

Chapter XVI

Śākyamuni Transmitted
Amida's Name to Śāriputra

Passages Relating How the Tathāgata Śākyamuni Kindly
Entrusted the Name of Amida to Śāriputra and Other Disciples

The *Amida Sutra* says:

> When the Buddha had finished teaching the sutra, Śāri-
> putra, the many monks, and the whole company of *devas*,
> men, and *asuras* from all over the world rejoiced greatly at
> having heard the Buddha's teaching. They accepted it, be-
> lieved in it, and bowed down in reverence before him and
> departed.

Shan-tao, explaining this passage in his *Liturgical Hymns*, says:

> The World-Honored One was teaching the Dharma, and at
> the very end of his discourse, he kindly entrusted the Name
> of Amida to his disciples. However, in an age when the Five
> Defilements are increasing, when doubts and slanders are
> many, and when both priests and laymen despise the
> Dharma, no one is ready to listen to this teaching. When
> they see anyone practicing, poisonous anger is aroused in
> them, and they subvert it with every available means. They
> vie with one another in arousing animosity against it. In
> this way, these *icchantika*s and people born blind inflict

131

damage on the Sudden Teaching and so remain submerged [in samsara] forever. Even after the lapse of as many kalpas as there are specks of dust in the whole universe, they will still not be able to extricate themselves from the Three Evil Realms. All sentient beings with one mind should repent all karmic sins of destroying the Dharma.

In my opinion, when we consider the broad intent of the three sutras, we can conclude that the most fundamental of all is to choose the Nembutsu from among the many forms of practice. First, in the *Two-Volume Sutra* there are three kinds of choosing: (1) it was chosen as [Amida's] Original Vow, (2) it was chosen through the special praise [of Śākyamuni], and (3) it alone was chosen to remain.

The first, "it was chosen as [Amida's] Original Vow," was the choice of the Nembutsu as the practice of Rebirth, which was selected by the monk Dharmākara from among all the practices in the twenty-one billion Buddha Lands. Above, we have examined its nature in detail. Therefore, it is said to have been "chosen as the Original Vow."

18c

The second is "it was chosen through special praise [of Śākyamuni]." Even though other practices, such as the awakening of the Bodhi mind, are described in the above quotation of passages concerning the three classes of people, nevertheless, Śākyamuni did not praise any of these other practices but praised only the Nembutsu, saying, "You should know that one utterance of the Nembutsu produces unsurpassable merit." That is why it is said to have been "chosen through the special praise [of Śākyamuni]."

The third is "it alone was chosen to remain." Although the other practices and the various good practices were mentioned above, Śākyamuni chose only the one method of the Nembutsu to remain. That is why it is said that "it alone was chosen to remain."

Next, the *Meditation Sutra* also mentions three ways of choosing. The first is choice by embracing. The second is that of Amida choosing [it] by praising [it] in his transformation body. The third is choice by entrusting [it] for transmission to future generations.

First, "choice by embracing" means that although the *Meditation Sutra* expounds the Contemplative and Distractive Practices, nevertheless, Amida's light shines only on those who practice the Nembutsu, embracing them and never abandoning them. Hence, this is called "choice by embracing."

Second, "choosing [it] by praising [it] in his transformation body" means that although the highest level of the lowest class of beings have the two practices of listening to the sutras and calling the Buddha's Name, nevertheless, the transformation body of Amida chooses the Nembutsu by saying to the practitioner, "Because you have uttered the Buddha's Name, all of your sins have vanished away, and I have come to welcome you." Hence, this is called "choosing [it] by praising [it] in his transformation body."

Third, "choice by entrusting" means that even though the many Contemplative and Distractive Practices were expounded, nevertheless, only the one practice of the Nembutsu was specially entrusted [to Ānanda by Śākyamuni]. That is why it is called "choosing by entrusting."

Next, in the *Amida Sutra* there is another type of choosing. It is choosing by witnessing [to its authenticity]. Although many sutras have expounded manifold practices for Rebirth, nevertheless, all the Buddhas of the six directions have not borne witness to these practices, but when the Nembutsu for Rebirth in the Pure Land is explained in this sutra, all the Buddhas of the six directions, as numerous as the sands of the Ganges, stretched forth their tongues throughout the great thousand-fold worlds and testified to the truth of this teaching. Hence, this is called "choosing by the act of witnessing to its authenticity."

In addition there is, in the *Sutra of the Samādhi Wherein All Buddhas Are Present*, the act of choosing known as "choosing my Name." Amida himself taught [it when he said,] "Those who wish to be reborn in my Land should choose to think continually of my Name without interruption." That is why it is known as "choosing my Name." These four [ways of choosing]—by the Original Vow, by embracing, by choosing my Name, and by praising [it] in his transformation body—are all choosings of Amida.

Three [ways of choosing]—by praise, by retention of the teaching [after other teachings disappear], and by entrusting—were all Śākyamuni's choosings.

Witnessing is the choice by all the Buddhas of the six directions, as numerous as the sands of the Ganges.

Therefore, both Śākyamuni and Amida, as well as all the Buddhas of the ten directions as numerous as the sands of the Ganges, have all with one mind chosen the single practice of the Nembutsu. This is not the case with the other practices. This is why one should clearly understand that all three of the sutras choose the Nembutsu and make it their principal teaching.

When I consider these matters carefully, I wish to urge that anyone who desires to escape quickly from the cycle of birth and death should decide between the two types of the excellent Dharma, lay aside the Holy Path for awhile, and choose to enter through the Gateway of the Pure Land. If such a person should desire to enter through the Gateway of the Pure Land, he or she should decide between the Right Practices and the Miscellaneous Practices, abandoning for awhile the various Miscellaneous Practices, and choose to take refuge in the Right Practices. If one desires to exercise oneself in the Right Practices, one should decide between the one Right Practice and the Auxiliary Right Practices, setting aside the Auxiliary Practices and resolutely choosing the act of Right Assurance and follow it exclusively. This act of Right Assurance is uttering the Name of Amida Buddha. Those who utter the Name will unfailingly attain Rebirth because it is based on Amida's Original Vow.

It may be asked, "The many masters of the Kegon, Tendai, Shingon, Zen, Sanron, and Hossō schools have each composed treatises and commentaries on the Dharma Gateway of the Pure Land. Why do you not rely on these masters, but use Shan-tao alone?"

My answer is that these other various masters, even though they all have written treatises and commentaries on the Pure Land, did not treat it as the central principle. They treated only the Holy Path as the central principle. This is the reason why I do not rely on these masters. Only the Master Shan-tao has treated the Pure

19a

134

Land as the central principle and has not so treated the Holy Path. This is why we rely solely on Shan-tao as our master.

It may further be asked, "The number of Pure Land Masters is great. For example, there are Chia-ts'ai of Hung-fa-ssu and Tripiṭaka Master Ts'u-min. Why do you never refer to these masters but rely on Shan-tao alone?" My reply is that although these teachers did indeed treat the Pure Land as the central principle, nevertheless, they were still not able to achieve Samādhi. Master Shan-tao was a man who did indeed achieve Samādhi. Precisely because he attained such a realization of the Way, we rely on him.

It may also be asked, "If then you rely on those who have been able to achieve Samādhi, the Dhyāna Master Huai-kan was a man who did attain it. Why do you not also rely on him?" My answer is that Shan-tao was the master, whereas Huai-kan was his disciple. One should rely on the master rather than on the disciple. Further, the master and his disciple differed in many points of doctrine. It is for these reasons that we do not rely on [the disciple].

Someone might further inquire, "If you rely on masters but not on their disciples, then since the Dhyāna Master Tao-ch'o was not only Master Shan-tao's own master but was also one of the patriarchs of the Pure Land School, why is it that you do not rely on him?"

I answer that although the Dhyāna Master Tao-ch'o was indeed Shan-tao's master, still he had not yet achieved Samādhi. That is why, when he himself did not know whether or not he could attain Rebirth, he asked Shan-tao, "Will my Nembutsu enable me to achieve Rebirth or not?" Shan-tao replied that he should take a single lotus blossom and place it before the Buddha's image and then practice the Pure Land Way for seven days. If the flower did not fade or wither, he would know clearly that his practice had assured him of Rebirth. Tao-ch'o acted in accord with these words and in fact, seven days later the flower had neither faded nor wilted.

In admiration of Shan-tao's deep realization, Tao-ch'o then asked him to enter into Samādhi in order to see if he would indeed

19b

finally attain Rebirth or not. Thereupon, Shan-tao did enter into Samādhi and in a very short time said in reply, "Master, you must first repent your three sins. Then you will surely be reborn. First, master, you long ago placed a precious statue of the Buddha under the eaves of the house in an outer room while you yourself occupied the main inner room. Second, you prodded your monks into a flurried pace of work. Third, in the course of constructing a building, you killed and injured worms. Master, you must properly repent of the first of these sins in the presence of the Buddhas of the ten directions. You must repent of the second sin before all the monks of the four directions. The third sin must be repented before all sentient beings."

Tao-ch'o quietly reflected upon his past misdeeds and admitted that indeed all of the accusations were true. Thereupon he purified his heart, repenting his guilt, and then he turned his gaze back to Shan-tao, who said to him, "Master, your sins have been obliterated. Hereafter, a ray of white light will surely envelop you. This, master, will be the sign of your Rebirth." (This record is found in the *Newly Compiled Record of Rebirth*.)

By these facts we know that Master Shan-tao achieved Samādhi in his practice and that his spiritual power was equal to that of his master. He was extraordinary both in his understanding and in his practice. This is a perfectly evident fact. Furthermore, his contemporaries passed on the following saying about him, "Since the Buddha's Dharma first came to the East, no one has equaled the great virtue of this Dhyāna Master. Who then can adequately describe his peerless fame?"

Furthermore, when he was compiling his commentary on the *Meditation Sutra*, he had profound experiences of spiritual portents, was often given teachings, and received divine guidance from the Holy Ones; and on the basis of this he accomplished the chapter division of the sutra. The whole world acclaimed it to be "the authorized commentary," and they held its teachings in equal esteem to those of the Buddha's sutras.

Thus at the end of the fourth volume of his *Commentary*, Shan-tao states:

I respectfully declare to all the masters with whom I enjoy karmic affinity: I am nothing more than an ordinary being caught up in the cycle of birth and death, one who is shallow in and short in wisdom. The teachings of the Buddha are profound and subtle, and one should not give rise to even a slight misunderstanding of them. Therefore I expressed the deep desire of my heart and made a firm vow asking for a sign of approval in the following manner, "I honor and take refuge in the Three Treasures, which fill the whole space of the Dharmadhātu, and also I take refuge in Śākyamuni, Amida, Avalokiteśvara, Mahāsthāmaprāpta, and in all the great sea of Bodhisattvas and in all of the ornamented aspects of the Pure Land. I now wish to set forth the essential meaning of the *Meditation Sutra* and to correct the misunderstandings of the masters from past times to the present. If this wish is in accord with the compassionate Vows of the many Buddhas of the Three Periods—Śākyamuni, Amida, and the rest—then please enable me to see in a dream all of the above desired aspects of the Pure Land."

After I made this vow before the image of the Buddha, I strengthened it by resolving with a sincere heart to recite the *Amida Sutra* three times and call to mind Amida Buddha thirty thousand times each day. And indeed that very night, I saw manifested in the western sky all of the aspects of the Pure Land mentioned above: hundreds and thousands of mountains made of precious stones of many colors, brilliant lights of all kinds illuminating the earth below, which was of a golden hue. In the midst of this sight were the Buddha and Bodhisattvas, some sitting, some standing, some speaking, some silent, some moving their bodies and hands, some remaining motionless. During this time, I had been standing with folded hands watching those aspects of the Pure Land. After a considerable period of time, I woke up.

Upon awaking I could not contain my joy, and thereupon 19c I forthwith noted down the essentials [of the *Meditation*

Sutra]. Thereafter, every night, a monk unfailingly came to me in a dream and taught me the chapter division of the Essential Meaning. After I had finished the work, I did not see him again.

After the book was finished, once again without fail I resolutely recited the *Amida Sutra* ten times, and called to mind Amida Buddha thirty thousand times every day for the fixed period of seven days. Each evening and again before dawn of these seven days, I contemplated the ornaments and other aspects of Amida's Pure Land, and I—exactly as before—took refuge in them with deep sincerity. During the course of that night I saw three stone mortar wheels turning of their own accord by the side of the road. Then suddenly a man came riding up on a white camel. He seemed to encourage me saying, "Master, you must certainly exert yourself with great resolve to achieve Rebirth. Take care lest you slip backward. This world is full of defilements, evil, and suffering. Do not get wrapped up in greed and pleasure." To this I gave answer, "I humbly accept the compassionate instruction of a being so full of wisdom. Until I die, I shall never dare to give way to laziness and pride."

On the second night I saw Amida Buddha, whose body was the color of purest gold, seated on a golden lotus beneath the tree of seven jewels. Around him sat ten monks, each under his own jewel tree. All over the Buddha's tree there was draped a heavenly cloth. I sat gazing on the scene with hands joined in reverence, directly facing the West.

On the third night, I saw two exceedingly tall flag poles from which hung five-colored banners. There were roads leading off in all directions from which one could observe the banners without obstruction.

After having had these revelations, I stopped my practice although the seven days had not yet been completed. My real intention in writing about all of the above holy revelations was for the benefit of others; it was not meant to benefit myself. Therefore once these revelations were received, I dare not keep them hidden. I respectfully state this after the exposition of the meaning [of the *Meditation Sutra*], hoping that it will be listened to by the people of future generations. My hope is that sentient beings, having heard this, will give birth to faith; that intelligent people who read the *Commentary* will take refuge in the Pure Land of the West.

I hereby transfer the merits of this work to all sentient beings so that all might awaken the Bodhi mind, face one another with compassionate hearts, and see one another with the eyes of the Buddha. May they as members of the household of Enlightenment become true spiritual friends. May they all together take refuge in the Pure Land and so together attain the Buddha's Way. These teachings were, upon my request, attested to and certified by the Buddhas. Not one phrase or one letter should be added or taken away from them. When anyone wishes to copy these words, let him do so in exactly the same manner as he would copy the sutras. This surely ought to be understood.

As I calmly reflect on these matters, it becomes clear that Shan-tao's *Commentary on the Meditation Sutra* is a guide to the Western Land and is the eyes and feet of practitioners. Therefore, whoever practices the Way of the Western Land should certainly hold it in the highest esteem. This is especially true in light of the fact that the monk who appeared nightly in a dream and instructed [Shan-tao] in the profound meanings of the sutra was most probably a transformation body of Amida himself. Hence it can be said that this *Commentary* is the direct exposition of Amida himself. Further, was it not commonly held during the great T'ang Dynasty that Shan-tao is Amida himself in the transformation body? And if such is the case, it may rightly be said that this book is the direct teaching of Amida himself. Then are not the above-cited words 20a the very truth: "When anyone wishes to copy these words, let him do so in exactly the same manner as he would copy the sutras"?

Should one wish to seek his original mode of being, it is none other than that of [Amida] the Dharma king of the Forty-eight Vows himself. The solemn pronouncement of the Supremely Enlightened One over ten kalpas ago is evidence that we can rely on the Nembutsu. Should one follow him down to his earthly manifestation, one finds that it was the master of the single-minded practice of the Nembutsu [Shan-tao]. The words that he accurately received in Samādhi leave no question about Rebirth. Although his forms differ in his original state and in his earthly manifestation, nevertheless he expounds a single way of salvation.

Long ago I, a monk of miserable accomplishment, chanced to read this book by Shan-tao and came to understand its meaning in a rough and general manner. Thereupon, I definitively abandoned the other practices and took refuge in the Nembutsu. From then on, up to the present day, both as my own practice and as my teaching to others, I have concentrated on the Nembutsu alone. During that time, when on rare occasions, I was asked about a fitting haven, I have always told them of the safe harbor of the Western Paradise. When occasionally I have been asked about religious practices, I have instructed the seekers in the special practice of the Nembutsu. Those who believed in my words have been many and those who refused them have been few. Hence, one should know that it is because the Pure Land teaching corresponds to the human capacity and the times, that it is now an opportune practice. The Nembutsu practice can be compared to the reflection of the moon in water: it freely rises up [to the moon] or [the moon] shines down [on the water].

Now, when I unexpectedly received a command to write this work, there were no grounds for refusing. Therefore, because of this command, I assembled this imperfect collection of essential passages on the Nembutsu and in addition explained its essential meaning. In doing so, I have not considered my own lack of talent but only the command I received. This, I confess, is an extremely improper and shameless thing.

I request that once Your Honor has deigned to read this work, you should hide it inside the bottom of a wall space, and certainly not leave it exposed in front of your window. This is because I fear that it may cause men who slander the Dharma to fall into evil ways.

Here concludes the *Collection of Passages on the Nembutsu Chosen in the Original Vow*.

Glossary

abhidharma (Jp. *abidatsuma*): A genre of literature that attempts systematic accounts of the whole body of early Buddhist teachings. One of the three divisions (*piṭakas*) (q.v.) of Buddhist scriptures. The term also refers to non-Mahayana schools such as Sarvāstivāda and Sautrāntika, which are often labeled as "inferior vehicles" (Hinayana) by Mahayanists. *See also* Tripiṭaka.

adornments of the two recompenses (Jp. *nihō shōgon*): The two recompenses (*nihō*) are Amida and his Pure Land. Adornments (*shōgon*) refer to the particularizations or concretizations of abstract or transcendent realities by means of symbols. In this way the manifestation of Amida and all adornments in his Pure Land can be understood to be symbolic concretizations of the "One Reality," i.e., of Emptiness. (q.v.).

Agada medicine (Jp. *akada-yaku*): A miraculous elixir that cures all ills.

almsgiving (Jp. *fuse*): One of the six *pāramitās* (q.v.).

Amida (Skt. Amitābha or Amitāyus): Amitābha means immeasurable light and Amitāyus means immeasurable life. The Name connotes the light of transcendental wisdom and universal compassion. According to the *Sutra of Immeasurable Life*, Amida Buddha, when he was Dharmākara Bodhisattva, made forty-eight vows to save all sentient beings and performed Bodhisattva practices to fulfill them. The Pure Land in the West, called Sukhāvatī (Jp. Gokuraku), is the fulfillment of his Vows and practice, in which even the most lowly who would think or meditate on him reach Buddhahood through his virtues.

Amida Sutra (T. 366, Skt. *Sukhāvatīvyūha*, Ch. *A-mi-t'a-ching*, Jp. *Amidakyō*): Translated by Kumārajīva. One of the three sutras of Pure Land Buddhism. The sutra briefly describes Amida's Pure Land and its virtues. It consists of a single volume and so is also often called "the shorter sutra" in Hōnen's text and elsewhere.

Anāgāmins (Jp. *nagon*): Sages who are not subject to return to this world of desire again, because their evil passions have been destroyed completely. They are in the third rank of Holy Persons (q.v.) on the path of *Śrāvaka*s (q.v.).

143

Arhats (Jp. *rakan*): Sages who have destroyed all the evil passions and are completely emancipated from the cycle of birth and death. They are in the fourth and highest rank of Holy Persons (q.v.) on the path of *Śrāvaka*s (q.v.).

artery (Jp. *kechimyaku*): Literally means a "blood vessel" or "artery." In all the Chinese and Japanese Buddhist sects, however, this "artery" refers to a genealogical table in which the direct line from the Buddha or the sect's or school's patriarchs is traced.

Auxiliary Acts (Jp. *jogō*): Acts to assist the practice of the Nembutsu. They are (1) chanting the sutras, (2) contemplating the adornments of Amida and his Pure Land, (3) worshipping Amida, (4) praising and making offerings to Amida. Part of the five Right Practices. *See also* Right Practice.

Auxiliary Practices (Jp. *jogyō*): Same as Auxiliary Acts (q.v.).

Avalokiteśvara (Jp. Kannon): The Bodhisattva of universal compassion. In the Pure Land sutras, Avalokiteśvara is one of the two attendants of Amida Buddha.

Avataṃsaka Sutra (Ch. *Hua-yen-ching*, Jp. *Kegonkyō*): A Mahayana sutra on which the teaching of the Kegon (Hua-yen) school is based. There are three Chinese translations, found in T. 278, T. 279, and T. 293.

biographies of eminent masters of the T'ang and Sung Dynasties (T. 2060, and T. 2061): There are two major collections of biographies of Buddhist masters, namely (1) the *Hsü* [or *T'ang*] *kao-seng-chuan* (Jp. *Zokukōsōden* or *Tōkōsōden*. T. 2060) in thirty fascicles, which contains biographies of masters from 521 to 647 c.e., and (2) the *Sung-kao-seng-chuan* (Jp. *Sōkōsōden*) in thirty fascicles, which contains biographies of T'ang Dynasty masters till 988 c.e.

Bodhi mind (Skt. *bodhicitta*, Jp. *bodaishin*): Aspiration for Enlightenment. Determination to follow the Bodhisattva path toward the attainment of one's own ultimate Enlightenment and for the sake of the salvation of all sentient beings.

Bodhi Mind Sutra (T. 307): Ch. *P'u-t'i-hsin-ching*, Jp. *Bodaishingyō*.

Bodhiruci (6th century): A Buddhist monk from north India. Arriving in Lo-yang, China, in 508, he translated many sutras and treatises, including Vasubhandu's *Treatise on the Sutra of Immeasurable Life*. He is reputed to have introduced T'an-luan to the Pure Land teaching by giving him a copy the *Meditation Sutra*.

Book of Filial Piety (Ch. *Hsiao-ching*, Jp. *Kōkyō*): A Confucian classic that teaches one's duties to one's parents.

burning house (Jp. *kataku*): A metaphor for this world, where people are tortured by the fire of their evil passions. One of the seven metaphors in the *Lotus Sutra*.

Candragarbha Sutra (Ch. *Ta-chi-yüeh-tsang-ching*, Jp. *Daijūgatsuzōkyō*): *Moon Storehouse Sutra*. The fifteenth section of the *Great Collection Sutra* (T. 397, Skt. *Mahāsaṃnipāta-sūtra*, Ch. *Ta-chi-ching*, Jp. *Daijikkyō*). This section of the sutra, which elaborates the theory of the decline of the Dharma after the demise of the Buddha, influenced the development of Tao-cho's view of the Age of the Dharma's Decadence. Hōnen's citation in Chapter 3, however, actually appears in the *Sūryagarbha Sutra* (*Sun Storehouse Sutra*, Ch. *Jih-tsang-ching*, Jp. *Nichizōkyō*), the fourteenth section of the *Mahāsaṃnipāta-sūtra*.

Chen-yüan Catalogue of Scriptures Contained in the Piṭakas (T. 2157, Jp. *Jōgen nyūzōroku*): A catalogue of Buddhist scriptures translated into Chinese compiled in 800, during the Chen-yüan (Jp. Jōgen) era in the T'ang Dynasty.

Collection of Passages on the Land of Peace and Bliss (T. 1958, Ch. *An-le-chi*, Jp. *Anrakushū*): A commentary on the *Meditation Sutra* that is Tao-ch'o's major work. One of Hōnen's major sources.

Collection of Passages on the Profound Meaning of the Mahayana (T. 1851, Ch. *Ta-ch'eng-i-chang*, Jp. *Daijōgishō*): A summary of Buddhist teachings written by Hui-yüan (Jp. Eon, 523–592).

Collection on the Essentials for Rebirth (T. 2682, Jp. *Ōjōyōshū*): Written by Genshin (942–1017). Hōnen originally became interested in Shan-tao's *Commentary on the Meditation Sutra* through this famous Japanese work.

Commentary on the Meditation Sutra (T. 1753, Ch. *Kuan-ching-shu*, Jp. *Kangyōsho*): A commentary on the *Meditation Sutra* in four volumes compiled by Shan-tao (613–681). Hōnen developed his Pure Land doctrines based on this work. The scriptural quotations in the *Senchakushū* are mostly from its first book, "Profound Meaning" (Jp. *Gengibun*), its third book, "The Contemplative Good Practices" (Jp. *Jōzengi*), and its fourth book, "The Distractive Good Practices" (Jp. *Sanzengi*).

Commentary on [Vasubandhu's] Treatise on Rebirth in the Pure Land (T. 1819, Ch. *Wang-sheng-lun-chu*, Jp. *Ōjōronchū*): A commentary on Vasubandhu's *Treatise on Rebirth in the Pure Land* compiled by T'an-luan (476–542). T'an-Luan harmoniously knitted together Mādhyamika and Yogācāra philosophy in his development of Vasubandhu's Pure Land teaching. His focus on Amida's Other Power and on the salvation of the lowest level of the lowest class of people constituted a major development in Chinese and Japanese Pure Land teaching. Shinran relied heavily on this important work.

Contemplative and Distractive Practices: Two goods, or two good practices, both lengthy and difficult practices referred to in the *Meditation Sutra*. Shan-tao discussed them in his *Commentary on the Meditation Sutra* in order to emphasize the importance of the Nembutsu, which he saw as superior to either. In the third and fourth books of his commentary, he declares that the first thirteen of the sixteen kinds of meditation on the Pure Land that the *Meditation Sutra* expounds (very long and difficult meditations on and visualizations of the beauties and wonders of Amida and his Pure Land) are the "Contemplative Practices," and the last three are the "Distractive Practices" or "practices for distracted people." At the end of the description of these two kinds of practices, he discusses the practice fit for very weak people, which is simply calling Amida to mind, especially at the hour of death. It is this practice that is described as the very center of the sutra, which is interpreted as recommending simply reciting the Nembutsu, even if only once. This is clearly not a literal interpretation of these practices in the *Meditation Sutra*. Shan-tao, however, in his deep reflections about the powerlessness of ordinary practitioners, argues strongly for this interpretation. He further maintains that all of the sixteen practices were actually meant to lead practitioners to the Nembutsu practice. Therefore these sixteen practices were really created only in order gradually to reveal the powerlessness of ordinary practitioners born in the Age of the Dharma's Decadence. Although they think that they can practice these meditations effectively, they actually are too weak to do so. As they come to realize their powerlessness, they too will come to rely solely on the Nembutsu. This notion is the central teaching of Chapter XII.

deep mind (Jp. *jinshin*): Mind of deep faith. Mind trusting in the power of the Amida's Original Vow. One of the Three Minds expounded in the *Meditation Sutra*. *See also* Three Minds.

dhāraṇī (Jp. *darani*, *sōji*, or *ju*): Dhāraṇis are formulas that contain the essence of the Buddha's teaching in short phrases and are believed to hold special power. They were originally in Sanskrit and then transliterated into Chinese and thence into Japanese, so that the original meanings, if any, were usually not known. Although in Hōnen's day they were often used merely as magic spells, Hōnen treats the Nembutsu as being the greatest of all the *dhāraṇi*s, which contains the essence of the teachings of the Buddha.

Dharma Gateway of Contemplation (T. 1959): Ch. *Kuan-nien-fa-men*, Jp. *Kannenbōmon*, by Shan-tao.

Dharma's Decadence (Jp. *mappō*): Last of the three periods after the Buddha's death. Although the teaching of the Buddha exists during this period, neither practices in accordance with the teaching nor Enlightenment in this world are possible any more. *See also* Periods of the Dharma.

earthly manifestation (Jp. *suishaku* or *suijaku*): Incarnations of Buddhas or Bodhisattvas in earthly forms. Shan-tao is believed to be an earthly incarnation of Amida.

eight grievous deeds (Jp. *hachijū*): Eight worst offences for Buddhist nuns. In addition to the four grievous deeds of (1) killing, (2) stealing, (3) carnal lust, and (4) lying, nuns will be expelled from the order if they (5) touch men's bodies, (6) do the following deeds with men, i.e., holding hands, touching clothes, staying in the same room, sitting together, walking together, nestling, and hoping to see him again, (7) withhold other persons' offences, and (8) breaking the rules to follow monks, and living together with monks. Nuns who commit these offences are to be expelled from the order.

eight kinds of guardians of Buddhism (Jp. *hachibu*): (1) Heavenly beings, (2) dragons, (3) *yakṣa*s (spirits), (4) *gandharva*s (gods of incense), (5) *asura*s (fighting spirits), (6) *garuḍa*s (heavenly birds that eat dragons), (7) *kiṃnara*s (gods of music), and (8) *mahoraga*s (serpent gods).

eight sections [in the *abhidharma*] (Jp. *hakkendo*): Sections that treat (1) karma, (2) bondage to the passions, (3) wisdom, (4) meditation, (5) the sense organs or "capacities" or "powers" (of the senses) as the "roots" of the disturbing passions, (6) elements, (7) views, and (8) miscellaneous.

eight storehouses (Jp. *hachizō*): (1) Womb-transformation storehouse (*taikezō*), (2) the storehouse of the intermediate stage between death and reincarnation (*chuinzō*), (3) the Mahayana-Vaipulya storehouse (*makaen-hōdōzō*), (4) the *śīla-vinaya*-storehouse (*kairitsuzō*), (5) the ten-stages storehouse (*jūjūzō*), (6) the miscellaneous storehouse (*zōzō*), (7) the diamond storehouse (*kongōzō*), and (8) the Buddha storehouse (*butsuzō*).

Emptiness (Skt. *śūnya*, or *śūnyatā*, Jp. *kū*): The idea that all phenomenal existences are "empty" of any sort of permanent entity. Hinayana schools teach that the concept of permanent "self" is a delusory idea. Mahayana schools further elaborate the idea by saying that not only "self" but all phenomenal existences are "empty." The theory of Emptiness became emphasized in Mahayana Buddhist thought, particularly in the Prajñāpāramitā literature. *See also* Middle Way.

Emptiness school (Jp. *musōshū*): The Sanron school, the Chinese version of the Indian Madhyamika, which emphasizes the emptiness of all phenomenal existences, and that ultimate truth itself is understood only through negations. *See also* Emptiness.

Eshin (942–1017): Another name for Genshin, the author of *The Collection on the Essentials for Rebirth* (*Ōjōyōshū*), which is one of the earliest and most influential works in the development of Japanese Pure Land thought.

Essentials for Rebirth in the Western Paradise (T. 1964, Ch. *Hsi-fang-yao-chüeh*, Jp. *Saihōyōketsu*): Attributed to Tz'u-en (Jp. Jion, 632–682).

Fa-chao (Jp. Hosshō, 8th century): Originator of *wu-hui* (*goe*) Nembutsu, intonation of the Nembutsu employing the five pitches of the Chinese musical scale. He was greatly influenced by Shan-tao.

Fa-shang (Jp. Hōjō, 495–580): An early Chinese Pure Land Master.

five aggregates (Jp. *goon*): (1) Matter, (2) sense perception, (3) mental conception, (4) volition, and (5) consciousness.

Five Bonds of the Higher Worlds of Form and Formlessness (Jp. *gojō*): (1) Attachment to form, (2) attachment to formlessness, (3) distraction of mind, (4) pride, and (5) ignorance.

five colors (Jp. *goshiki*): The primary colors, white, black, red, yellow, and blue. They represent religious ideals. In some accounts, white represents faith; red, zeal; yellow, memory; blue, meditation; and black, wisdom.

Five Corruptions (Jp. *gojoku*): (1) Corruption of the time, that is, a degenerate age, full of calamities (*kōjoku*), (2) corruption of thought or belief, i.e., people have wrong ideas and superstitions (*kenjoku*), (3) corruption of feeling, i.e., people are full of evil passions (*bonnōjoku*), (4) corruption of the person, i.e., people('s) bodies become weak and their characters degenerate (*shujōjoku*), and (5) corruption of life, i.e., people's lives are shortened (*myōjoku*).

five deadly sins (Jp. *gogyaku*): Five offences that create the causes of falling into the Avīci hell, the hell of interminable pain. They are (1) killing one's father, (2) killing one's mother, (3) killing an Arhat, (4) causing a Buddha's body to bleed, and (5) disturbing the harmony of the Buddhist order.

five groups of Dharma gateways (Jp. *goju no hōmon*): Five divisions of the Buddhist doctrine in the *Collection of Passages on the Profound Meaning of the Mahayana*. They are (1) Teaching of the Dharma Gateways, (2) Meanings, (3) Defilements, (4) Pure Things, and (5) Miscellaneous.

five kinds of Dharma Masters (Jp. *goshu hōshi*): Five kinds of Dharma Masters mentioned in the *Lotus Sutra*. They are (1) one who holds the sutra, (2) one who reads and chants it, (3) one who learns it by heart, (4) one who expounds it to others, and (5) one who copies it.

five kinds of esteem and praise (Jp. *goshu no kayo*): Refers to the passage in Chapter XI, "Whoever recites the Nembutsu is a most excellent, wonderful good, and a person of the highest level of the superior class, and the rarest and most excellent of all people"

five kinds of Right Practice (Jp. *goshu shōgyō*): Five Right Practices to attain birth in the Pure Land systematized in Shan-tao's *Commentary on the Meditation Sutra*. They are (1) chanting the sutras, (2) contemplating the adornments of Amida and his Pure Land, (3) worshipping Amida, (4) recitation of the Name of Amida, and (5) praising and making offerings to Amida. Shan-tao states that the recitation of the Name is the Right Established Act for the birth in Pure Land, and that the rest are Auxiliary Acts to assist the practice. *See also* Right Practice, Right Established Act, and Auxiliary Acts.

Five Precepts (Jp. *gokai*): Five precepts for the lay practitioners to follow. They are (1) not to kill, (2) not to steal, (3) not to commit adultery, (4) not to lie, and (5) not to drink intoxicating liquors.

five sufferings (Jp. *goku*): Five kinds of suffering in human life. They are (1) birth, (2) aging, (3) sickness, (4) death, and (5) parting from loved ones.

Five Supernatural Powers (Jp. *gojinzū*): The power (1) to see anything in the universe, (2) to hear any sound, (3) to know all the thoughts of other minds, (4) to know all of one's own and others' previous lives in other incarnations, and (5) to be anywhere to do anything at will. Amida vowed in the Fifth through the Ninth of the Forty-eight Vows that these supernatural powers would be attained by all those reborn in his Pure Land.

Five Tone Ceremonial Hymns (T. 1983, Ch. *Wu-hui-fa-shih-tsan*, Jp. *Goehōji-san*): A collection of hymns that were compiled by Fa-chao (Jp. Hosshō, 8th century c.e.) using five pitches. These beautiful renderings were used as a means of preaching the Pure Land teachings.

four *Āgamas* (Jp. *shiagon*): Early Buddhist scriptures, divided into four groups, corresponding to four of the five *Nikāyas* (collections) of the Pali Canon: (1) *Dīghanikāya* (Jp. *Jōagon*), (2) *Majjhimanikāya* (Jp. *Chūagon*), (3) *Saṃyuttanikāya* (Jp. *Zōagon*), and (4) *Aṅguttaranikāya* (Jp. *Zōitsuagon*).

four boundless minds (Jp. *shimuryōshin*): Four minds for benefitting others. They are (1) boundless love, (2) boundless compassion, (3) boundless joy, and (4) boundless equanimity or indifference.

four elements (Jp. *shidai*): Four constituent elements in phenomenal world. They are (1) earth, (2) water, (3) fire, and (4) air.

four fearlessnesses (Jp. *shimui*): A Buddha is free from all sorts of fear (1) because he has all knowledge, (2) because he has all freedom, (3) because he is able to show people all the obstructions in the way of their deliverance, and (4) because he is able to teach people the true way to nirvana.

four grades of holy people (Jp. *shishō*): *Śrāvaka* (q.v.), *Pratyekabuddha* (q.v.), Bodhisattva, and Buddha. For another four, *see* Holy Persons.

four grievous deeds (Jp. *shijū*): The four most grave offences for Buddhist monks and nuns. (1) Killing, (2) stealing, (3) carnal lust, and (4) lying. Those who commit these offences are to be expelled from the order.

Four Modes of Practice (Jp. *shishu*): (1) The practice of veneration, (2) exclusive practice [of the Nembutsu], (3) uninterrupted practice, and (4) long-term practice [for all of one's life]. These modes were already familiar in other sects, but they are given special meaning in this text.

four things (Jp. *shiji*): Four kinds of offerings. They are (1) clothing, (2) food and drink, (3) bedding, and (4) medicine.

Four Treatises (Jp. *shiron*): Four essential commentaries elaborating the theory of Emptiness. They are the (1) *Mādhyamika-śāstra* (Jp. *Chūron*), (2) *Śata-śāstra* (Jp. *Hyakuron*), (3) *Dvadaśamukhaśāstra* (Jp. *Jūnimonron*), and (4) *Mahāprajñāpāramitāśāstra* (Jp. *Chidoron*), the fundamental scriptures of the Four Treatises school.

four universal vows (Jp. *shiguzeigan*): Four universal vows shared by all Buddhas and Bodhisattvas. They are (1) to save all of the countless living beings, (2) to put an end to inexhaustible evil passions, (3) to learn all of the innumerable gateways to the Dharma, and (4) to attain the incomparable Buddha Way.

Four Vehicles: Four Buddhist paths, or teachings. They are Vehicles of the *Śrāvaka*s (q.v.), *Pratyekabuddha*s (q.v.), Bodhisattvas, and Buddhas.

four wisdoms (Jp. *shichi*): The four forms of transformed consciousness discussed in the Yogācāra or Hossō school. They are (1) the mirror wisdom (Skt. *ādarśa-jñāna*, Jp. *daienkyōchi*), (2) the wisdom of equality (Skt. *samatājñāna*, Jp. *byōdōshōchi*) (3) the wisdom of wondrous perception (Skt. *pratyavekṣanā-jñāna*, Jp. *myōkanzatsuchi*), and (4) the wisdom of accomplishing metamorphoses into different forms and states of being (Skt. *kṛtyānuṣṭhāna-jñāna*, Jp. *jōshosachi*). These wisdoms emerge from the eight forms of consciousness when illusion is destroyed and Enlightenment is realized.

Gateway of the Holy Path (Ch. *sheng-tao-men*, Jp. *shōdōmon*): The Buddhist path of sages, both Hinayana and Mahayana, who practice to attain Enlightenment in this world by their own power. Tao-ch'o maintains that the Holy Path is not suitable for people in the Age of the Dharma's Decadence, so that all people in this present age should follow the Gateway of the Pure Land through the Nembutsu practice. *See* Gateway of the Pure Land.

Gateway of the Pure Land (Ch. *ching-t'u-men*, Jp. *jōdomon*): The Buddhist path to attain birth in the Pure Land. Opposite of the Gateway of the Holy Path. By entrusting oneself to the power of Amida's Vow, one will attain birth in the Pure Land, where one will attain Enlightenment.

great guardian kings of the four directions (Jp. *shiten daiō*): Kings of the four heavenly realms around Mount Sumeru in the center of the cosmos. They are (1) Dhṛtarāṣṭra in the east, (2) Virūḍhaka in the south, (3) Virūpākṣa in the west, and (4) Vaiśravaṇa in the north. While serving the god Indra, they protect Buddhism and its believers.

Holy Path (Jp. Shōdō): The Way of sages, both Hinayana and Mahayana, who engage in ascetic practice in this world in order to attain Enlightenment. Hōnen groups all those Buddhist schools that rely on ascetic practice into this category. Only those who rely solely on the Nembutsu and the performance of the other Auxiliary Practices related to honoring Amida are not included in this Holy Path. *See* Gateway of the Holy Path.

Holy Persons: *Srotāpanna*s, *Sakṛdāgamin*s, *Anāgāmin*s (q.v.), and Arhats (q.v.). *Srotāpanna*s are those who have just entered the stream of holiness, and *Sakṛdāgamin*s are those who will be born in the world of desire just once more before attaining Enlightenment.

Huai-kan, Dharma Master (Jp. Ekan): A disciple of Shan-tao who lived in the seventh and eighth centuries. He wrote *The Treatise on Clearing Up Many Doubts* (T. 1960, Ch. *Ch'ün-i-lun*, Jp. *Gungiron*).

Hui-ch'ung (Jp. Echō): He is listed as the second Dharma Master in the *Collection of Passages on the Land of Peace and Bliss*, but nothing is known about his life, and his dates are unclear.

Hui-yüan of Lu-shan (334–416, Jp. Rozan no Eon): He established the White Lotus Society on Mount Lu for the performance of meditation on Amida.

Hymns in Praise of Rebirth (T. 1980, Ch. *Wan-sheng-li-tsan*, Jp. *Ōjōraisan*): By Shan-tao. These very beautiful hymns, like the other major works of Shan-tao, greatly influenced Hōnen. They are still often chanted by his followers. It is popularly called "The Six Times a Day Hymn of Praise" (*Rokuji raisan*) because it is chanted six times a day.

*icchantika*s (Jp. *sendai*): People who do not have the root of goodness and therefore can never become Buddhas by their own power. Pure Land Buddhism teaches that even *icchantika*s can be reborn into Pure Land through the power of Amida's Vow and attain Enlightenment.

Idealist school (Jp. *Usōshū*): The Hossō school. This school holds the doctrinal position that all phenomena are manifestations of the aspects of consciousness.

kalpa (Jp. *kō*): An extremely long period of time. The length of this period is so great that it can only be explained by metaphors, such as the time it would take for a mountain of granite a hundred cubic *yojana*s in volume (one *yojana* ≈ 12 English miles) to be worn away by a heavenly spirit flying over it once in a hundred years and touching it gently with its sleeves; or the time needed for a person of very long life to come once every one hundred years, and carry off one grain of sand from a mountain one hundred cubic *yojana*s in volume until he removed the entire mountain.

King of Teachings (Ch. *Chiao-wang*, Jp. *Kyō-ō*): The *Diamond Crown Sutra* (T. 874, Ch. *chin-kang-ting-ching*, Jp. *Kongōchōkyō*). One of the three sutras of the Shingon school.

Larger Amida Sūtra (T. 362, Ch. *Ta-a-mi'ta-ching*, Jp. *Dai Amidakyō*): An alternative Chinese translation of the *Sutra of Immeasurable Life* (q.v.). *See also* Threefold Sutra of the Pure Land.

Larger Prajñāpāramitā Sūtra (T. 220): Ch. *Ta-po-jo-ching*, Jp. *Dai hannyakyō*.

Light Heart in the Way of Peace and Bliss (T. 1965): Ch. *Yu-hsin-an-le-tao*, Jp. *Yushin anrakudō*. Compiled by Wŏn Hyo (617–686, Jp. Gangyō), a Korean scholar of the Hua-yen (Jp. Kegon) school and a Pure Land Master.

Liturgical Hymns (T. 1979): Ch. *Fa-shih-tsan*, Jp. *Hōjisan*. Compiled by Shan-tao.

Lotus Sutra (T. 262, Ch. *Fa-hua-ching*, Jp. *Hoke-kyō*, Skt. *Saddharma-puṇḍarīka-sutra*): Mahayana sutra on which the T'ien-tai (Jp. Tendai) and Nichiren schools are based. Although this well-known Mahayana sutra discusses Rebirth in the Pure Land only incidentally, according to the *Meditation Sutra*, the reading and recitation of this sutra can be a practice leading to Rebirth. However, Shan-tao (and Hōnen) say that reading and recitation of Mahayana sutras such as this one is a Distractive Practice and so should be cast aside in favor of the Nembutsu.

Mahāsthāmaprāpta (Jp. Seishi): The Bodhisattva of universal wisdom. In the Pure Land sutras, Mahāsthāmaprāpta is one of the two attendants of Amida Buddha.

major and minor bodily characteristics (Jp. *sōgō*): The body of a Buddha has thirty-two special major and eighty minor marks.

Meaning of the Bodhi Mind (T. 1953): Ch. *P'u-t'i-hsin-i*, Jp. *Bodaishingi*.

Meditation Sutra (T. 365, *Kuan-ching*, Jp. *Kangyō*): One of the sutras in the Threefold Sutra of the Pure Land. The full title is *The Sutra of Meditation on the Buddha of Immeasurable Life* (Ch. *Kuan-wu-liang-shou-ching*, Jp. *Kanmuryōjukyō*). This sutra elaborates sixteen contemplations on Amida and the Pure Land. Shan-tao's commentary on this sutra,

Commentary on the Meditation Sutra (q.v.), is the most influential on Hōnen's theory of Nembutsu practice.

Middle Way (Skt. *madhyamā pratipad*, Jp. *chūdō*): The doctrine of non-duality. The right path toward Enlightenment, which is beyond extreme views, and which sees all phenomenal presences as neither suffering nor joy, neither existent nor non-existent, and neither eternal nor temporary; they exist only interdependently.

mind that desires to transfer [merit towards being born in Amida's Pure Land] (Jp. *ekōhotsuganshin*): Mind aspiring to be born in Amida's Pure Land. One of the Three Minds expounded in the *Meditation Sutra*. *See also* Three Minds.

Miscellaneous Practice (Jp. *zōgyō*): Practices for birth in the Pure Land; opposites of the Right Practice (q.v.). Applying the meritorious practices of the Gateway of the Holy Path (q.v.), or practices for Buddhas, Bodhisattvas, and holy beings other than Amida, for the sake of one's birth in the Pure Land.

Nāgārjuna (ca. 150–250): Established the foundation of the Mādhyamika school. He is also traditionally respected as the founder of Mahayana Buddhism. In Japan, he is often referred to as the patriarch of all of the eight schools Buddhism introduced from China.

nayuta: Signifies a very large number, about a hundred million.

Nembutsu (Ch. *Nien-fo*, Jp. *Nenbutsu*): Literally "Remembering (or Calling to Mind) the Buddha." This meaning is derived from the original Pure Land notions such as those described in the *Meditation Sutra*. The term also came to mean the uttering of the Name of Amida in the phrase, "Namu Amida Butsu (I take refuge in Amida Buddha)." *See also* Contemplative and Distractive Practices; Original Vow.

Newly Compiled Record of Rebirth: Ch. *Hsin-hsiu-wang-sheng-chuan*, Jp. *Shinshū ōjōden*.

nine classes of people (Ch. *chiu-p'in*, Jp. *kubon*): Nine grades of birth in the Pure Land described in the *Meditation Sutra*. There are three classes: (1) upper class (Jp. *jōbon*) (2) middle class (Jp. *chūbon*), and (3) lower class (*gebon*). This classification is further subdivided into three grades: (1) upper birth (*jōshō*), (2) middle birth (*chūshō*), and (3) lower birth (*geshō*) in each class. According to the *Meditation Sutra*, the birth of aspirants to the Pure Land is classified into a total of nine levels according to the practices and virtues accumulated in their previous lives. *See also* three classes of people.

Nirvana Sutra (T. 374): Ch. *Nieh-p'an-ching*, Jp. *Nehangyō*. Also called *Mahā-parinirvāṇa-sūtra*.

original mode of being (Jp. *honji*): Buddhas and Bodhisattvas in their original celestial modes of being also manifest as incarnations in earthly
form. Hōnen considers Shan-tao an incarnation of Amida Buddha.

Original Vow (Skt. *pūrva-praṇidhāna*, Jp. *hongan*): The Bodhisattva's vow
made at the beginning of his spiritual career. In the Pure Land teaching, this refers to Amida's Vow made when he was Dharmākara
Bodhisattva. The Chinese Pure Land Master Shan-tao, and Hōnen, who
closely followed his teaching, selected the Eighteenth Vow in the *Sutra
of Immeasurable Life* as the most essential vow for the salvation of sentient beings. Shan-tao particularly focused on the Eighteenth Vow because it guaranteed Rebirth in the Pure Land to all those who sincerely
call to mind Amida and his Land. Shan-tao's predecessor, Tao-ch'o, following the *Meditation Sutra*, declared that this Vow brings Rebirth even
to the worst sinners who have never engaged in good deeds of any kind,
provided that they meditate on Amida up to ten times when they are
dying. Shan-tao further simplified the practice by interpreting the Vow
to require reciting the Name of Amida. In the *Senchakushū*, Hōnen
makes a strong case for the interpretation that recitation of the Name,
even once, is the one and only central and necessary practice. This was
the final radical simplification that brought Buddhist practice within
the range of the tastes and capabilities of ordinary people. Perhaps no
other single teaching was so influential in bringing Buddhism into the
minds and hearts of the Japanese people and into their culture.

Other Power (Ch. *t'o-li*, Jp. *tariki*): The power of Amida's Original Vow.
Amida's salvific activities to emancipate all sentient beings. The notion
of Other Power was first given prominence in T'an-luan's *Commentary
on [Vasubandhu's] Treatise on Rebirth in the Pure Land* (q.v.). People
cannot be enlightened by their own efforts and practices in the Age of
the Dharma's Decadence, but practice of the Nembutsu is made available to them through Amida's compassionate Vows. Those who aspire
to be born in the Pure Land need only call the Name of Amida. The
concept is a simple one but has proved to be of incalculable power in the
history of Japanese Buddhism. *See also* self power.

*pāramitā*s: The six major virtues of the Bodhisattva; almsgiving, observance
of the precepts, patience, zeal, meditation, and wisdom.

Passages Concerning the Pure Land (T. 1970): Ch. *Ching-t'u-wen*, Jp.
Jōdomon. Compiled by Wang-jih-hsiu (Jp. Ō Nikkyū, d. 1173) of Lung-
shu (Jp. Ryūjo).

Path of Insight and Path of Practice (Jp. *kentai shudō*): The first two of the
three stages in the Path of the Śrāvakas. The Path of Insight (Jp. *kendō*)
is to awaken to the reality of the four noble truths for the first time. The

Path of Practice (Jp. *shudō*) is to cultivate the insight continuously, which will lead practitioners to the last stage where nothing remains to be cultivated (Jp. *mugakudō*).

Periods of the Dharma: Three periods after the Buddha's demise. They are (1) the Period (or Age) of the Right Dharma, wherein people can still achieve Enlightenment through their own efforts, (2) the Period of the Semblance of the Dharma, wherein both the Dharma and practice still exist but people can no longer achieve Enlightenment, and (3) the Period of the Dharma's Decadence, wherein the Dharma still exists but there is neither strenuous practice nor Enlightenment. There are many differing versions of the Ages or Periods following the death of Śākyamuni. Tao-ch'o (562–645) used a threefold division of these ages which subsequently became the standard one in Pure Land thought. There were various theories as to the length of these three ages, but in Tao-ch'o's day the most common one was that the first period lasted five hundred years, the second a thousand years, and the third, which we are presently in, would last ten thousand years. This notion that the world is now in the "latter age" (Jp. *mappō*) became immensely popular in medieval Japan, appearing very often even in secular literature.

piṭaka: Basket or collection of written works. *See also* Tripiṭaka.

Pratyekabuddha (Jp. *engaku*): A sage who attains Enlightenment by observing the principle of causation by himself. He attains emancipation without the guidance of a teacher and he intends neither to guide others nor to expound the teaching to others. One of the two kinds of Hinayana sages. See also *Śrāvaka*.

Realist school: The Kusha school, which was founded on the teaching of the *Abhidharmakośa* (Ch. *A-p'i-ta-mo-chü-shê-lun*, Jp. *Abidatsuma kusharon*, T. 1558). The *Abhidharmakośa* is a comprehensive treatise discussing the Hinayana doctrine, compiled by Vasubandhu. See also *abhidharma*; Vasubandhu.

Records of the Lines of the Dharma Transmission (Jp. *Buppō kechimyakufu*): Compiled by Saichō (767–822). The full title is *Naishō buppō sōjō kechimyakufu*.

reflection of the moon in water: The moon is likened to Amida, and water to the Nembutsu practitioner. The moon is able to be visually present in water without really leaving the sky, just as Amida can be present to the Nembutsu practitioner through his Vow without leaving the Pure Land.

Right Established Act (Jp. *shōjōgō*): Practice of the recitation of the Nembutsu, which certainly assures one of birth in the Pure Land. One of the five Right Practices. *See* Right Practice.

Right Practice: Practice leading to birth in the Pure Land. Opposite of Miscellaneous Practice (q.v.). Shan-tao distinguished the following five kinds of practice: (1) chanting the three Pure Land sutras, (2) contemplating Amida and his Land, (3) doing reverence to Amida, (4) recitation of Amida's Name, and (5) praising Amida's merits. Shan-tao identified the recitation of Amida's Name, or Nembutsu practice, as the Right Established Act (Jp. *shōjōgō*). He called the rest Auxiliary Acts (Jp. *jogō*), which assist the Nembutsu practice. Chapter Two of the *Senchakushū* is given over entirely to delineating the Right from other Miscellaneous Practices in such a way as to point up the superiority of the Nembutsu. *See* Miscellaneous Practice.

Saha world (Jp. *shaba*): Sahā is a Sanskrit term meaning "enduring" and refers to the ordinary world in which one must endure suffering.

samādhi (Jp. *sanmai*): A mental state of concentration and focusing of thought on one object.

Samantabhadra Meditation Sutra (T. 277): Ch. *P'u-hsien-kuan-ching*, Jp. *Fugenkangyō*.

Śāriputra (Jp. Sharihotsu): One of the ten great disciples of the Buddha. He was renowned for his intelligence.

Satyasiddhi [school] (Ch. *Ch'eng-shih*, Jp. *Jōjitsu*): Chinese version of the Sautrāntika school, founded on the *Satyasiddhi-śāstra* (T. 1646, Ch. *Ch'eng-shih-lun*, Jp. *Jōjitsuron*) of Harivarman (ca. 250–350).

self power (Ch. *tzu-li*, Jp. *jiriki*): The practitioner's own power to reach Enlightenment. Opposite of Other Power (q.v.) Aspiring to be born in the Pure Land by cultivating virtues by one's own efforts.

Shan-tao (613–681, Jp. Zendō): One of the five Pure Land patriarchs and Tao-cho's successor. He established the Pure Land teaching in the early T'ang Dynasty, and was the Chinese patriarch on whom Hōnen relied most heavily in his works, especially his use of Shan-tao's *Commentary on the Meditation Sutra* (q.v.).

Shao-k'ang (d. 805): One of the five Chinese Pure Land patriarchs. Popularly known as "the incarnation of Shan-tao."

six acts of mindfulness (Jp. *rokunen*): Thinking of the Buddha, the Dharma, the Sangha, the precepts, almsgiving, and heaven.

six directions (Jp. *roppō*): East, south, west, north, below, and above.

six forms of consciousness (Jp. *rokushiki*): Sight, hearing, smell, taste, touch, and thought.

six objects (Jp. *rokujin*): Color and form, sound, smell, taste, the feel of things, and the characteristics of things known to the mind.

six organs of sense (Jp. *rokkon*): The eyes, the ears, the nose, the tongue, the body, and the mind.

six realms (Jp. *rokudō*): The realms of the (1) hells, (2) hungry ghosts, (3) animals, (4) fighting demons, (5) humans, and (6) heavenly beings.

Śramaṇa (Jp. *shamon*): A religious mendicant who has left his home and taken up the ascetic life seeking salvation. A Buddhist monk.

Śrāvaka (Jp. *shōmon*): A hearer of [the Buddha's] voice. Direct disciples of the Buddha. Later Mahayanists began using this word to criticize the followers of the Hinayana, saying that they seek Enlightenment for themselves and do not think of enlightening others. One of the two kinds of Hinayana sages. See also *Pratyekabuddha*.

Stage of Non-Retrogression (Skt. *avaivartika* or *avinivartanīya*, Jp. *abibacchi*, or *futaiten*): The step Bodhisattvas reach where they are assured of eventual Enlightenment without falling back to lower spiritual stages, because their understanding of the Way is so deep that it is impossible for them to be deceived by deluded ideas and illusions. In Hōnen's Pure Land school, those who attain birth in the Pure Land are at this stage.

Stage of Right (or Genuine) Assurance (Jp. *shōjōju*): The stage Bodhisattvas reach from which entrance into nirvana is assured. For Pure Land followers, this is the stage where one's Rebirth is assured. *See also* Stage of Non-Retrogression.

Sudden Teaching (Jp. *tongyō*): Higher teaching that directly reveals the ultimate truth. Teaching that enables practitioners to attain Enlightenment swiftly. Opposite of Gradual Teaching (Jp. *zenkyō*). The teaching of the Nembutsu is a Sudden Teaching because it states that if one recites the Nembutsu even once, one will immediately attain the condition necessary for Rebirth.

sutra(s): Discourses or sermons delivered by the Buddha. They have a special format, beginning with the words, "Thus have I heard, at one time..." One of the three divisions (*piṭaka*s) (q.v.) of Buddhist scriptures. Due to the emphasis on Dharma (the truth rediscovered by the Buddha), rather than on the Buddha himself and his words, the Buddha's words have been, without hesitation, re-interpreted and rewritten over the centuries. *See also* Tripiṭaka.

Sutra at the King's Palace: The *Meditation Sutra* (q.v.) which was expounded at the palace in the city of Rājagṛha.

Sutra of Avalokiteśvara's Prediction (T. 371): Ch. *Kuan-yin-shou-chi-ching*, Jp. *Kannon-jukikyō*.

Sutra of Correct Dharma Thought (T. 721): Ch. *Cheng-fa-nien-ching*, Jp. *Shōbōnengyō*.

Sutra of Immeasurable Life (T. 360, Skt. *Sukhāvatīvyūha*, Ch. *Wu-liang-shou-ching*, Jp. *Muryojukyō*): One of the Threefold Sutras of the Pure Land (q.v.) identified by Hōnen. The sutra elaborates how Amida's Original Vows have been accomplished and how sentient beings can to be born in the Pure Land. This sutra is also known as the *Larger Sūtra*. As a convenient distinction the character for "large" (*dai*) is often placed in front of the Japanese name, *Daimuryojokyō*. It consists of two volumes and so sometimes is referred to as the *Two-Volume Sutra*. In addition to the most popular translation of the sutra attributed to Saṃghavarman (Ch. *K'ang-Seng-k'ai*, Jp. *Kōsōgai*), there are four alternative Chinese translations (T. 361, 362, 363, and 310, Section 5). Hōnen quotes two of these in the *Senchakushū* (Ch. 3): the *Larger Amida Sutra* (q.v.) and the *Sutra of Universal Enlightenment* (q.v.).

Sutra of Infinite Meaning (T. 276): Ch. *Wu-liang-i-ching*, Jp. *Muryōgikyō*.

Sutra of Maitreya's Ascending Birth (T. 452): Ch. *Shang-sheng-ching*, Jp. *Jōshōkyō*.

Sutra of Meditation on Mind (T. 159): Ch. *Hsin-ti-kuan-ching*, Jp. *Shinji kangyō*.

Sutra of the Dharma's Eternal Dwelling (T. 819): Ch. *Fa-ch'ang-chu-ching*, Jp. *Hōjōjūkyō*.

Sutra of the Samādhi Wherein All the Buddhas Are Present (T. 418): Ch. *Pan-chou-san-mei-ching*, Jp. *Hanjuzammaikyō*.

Sutra of the Six Pāramitās (T. 261): Ch. *Liu-po-lo-mi-ching*, Jp. *Ropparamitsukyō*.

Sutra of the Ten Rebirths (in *Zokuzōkyō* 1. 87. 4): Ch. *Shih-wang-sheng-ching*, Jp. *Jūōjōkyō*.

Sutra of Universal Enlightenment (T. 361): Ch. *Ping-teng-chüeh-ching*, Jp. *Byōdōgakukyō*. An alternate translation of the *Sutra of Immeasurable Life*.

Sutra on the Dhāraṇī of the Drum's Sound (T. 370): Ch. *Ku-yin-sheng-t'o-lo-ni-ching*, Jp. *Kuonjō-Daranikyō*.

Ta-hai (Jp. *Daikai*, 541–609): A Chinese Pure Land Dhyāna Master.

T'an-luan (476–542, Jp. Donran): One of the five Chinese Pure Land patriarchs. At first, he was a scholar of the Shiron, or Four Treatises (q.v.) school. According to the tradition, he converted to the Pure Land teachings immediately after he received the import of the *Meditation Sutra* from Bodhiruci (q.v.). T'an-luan was the author of the *Commentary on [Vasubandhu's] Treatise on Rebirth in the Pure Land* (q.v.).

Tao-ch'ang (Jp. Dōjō, date not known): A Chinese Pure Land Dharma Master.

Tao-ch'o (562–645, Jp. Dōshaku): One of the Pure Land patriarchs in China. He was at first a scholar of the *Nirvana Sutra* but later turned to the Pure Land Teachings. He wrote the *Collection of Passages on the Land of Peace and Bliss* (q.v.), in which he first made the important distinction between the Gateways of the Holy Path and the Pure Land.

teachings which only incidentally expound Rebirth in the Pure Land: The text mentions this category of sacred Buddhist texts, which includes "the sutras which expound Rebirth in the Pure Land, such as the *Garland Sutra*, the *Lotus Sutra*, the *Wish-fulfilling Dhāraṇi Sutra*, the *Dhāraṇi Sutra on the Most August One*, and others [and also] treatises, such as the *Awakening of Faith*, the *Treatise on the Precious Nature*, the *Treatise Explaining the Ten Stages*, the *Compendium of the Mahayana*, and similar works that expound Rebirth in the Pure Land." Hōnen makes a powerful argument against his opponents from other Buddhist groups of his day by using his great erudition to list this large numbers of texts—many of which were well regarded by his opponents—in which the Pure Land school was treated as an important tradition.

ten directions (Jp. *jippō*): The eight points of the compass, which are the four directions, plus northwest, etc., plus the nadir and the zenith.

ten evils (Jp. *jūaku*): Killing, stealing, adultery, lying, duplicity, coarse language, covetousness, greed, anger, and perverted views.

ten goods (Jp. *jūzen*): The acts of refraining from the ten evils. *See also* ten evils.

ten headings (Jp. *jikka*): (1) Translating sutras, (2) understanding the meaning of sutras, (3) practicing meditating, (4) explaining the Vinaya (q.v.), (5) protecting the Dharma, (6) supernatural powers, (7) venerating relics, (8) reading and reciting the sutras, (9) amassing proper merit, and (10) miscellaneous.

ten kinds of Dharma practice (Jp. *jisshu hōgyō*): (1) Copying the sutras, (2) reverencing them, (3) propagating the teaching of sutras, (4) listening to them, (5) reading them, (6) memorizing them, (7) explaining them, (8) reciting them, (9) contemplating their meaning, and (10) putting their teachings into practice.

ten powers (Jp. *jūriki*): The ten powers of a Buddha, which give perfect knowledge of (1) right and wrong, (2) the karmic condition of every being, past, present, and future, (3) all stages of *dhyāna* and *samādhi*, (4) the faculties of all beings, (5) the desires of every being, (6) the actual condition of every individual, (7) the direction and consequence of all acts, (8) all causes of mortality and of good and evil, (9) the final end of all beings and their nirvana, and (10) how to destroy all illusions of every kind.

Ten Stages of the Bodhisattva (Jp. *jūji*): In the fifty-two stages of the Bodhisattva's career, this corresponds to the forty-first to fiftieth stages. When a Bodhisattva has reached the first of the ten stages, he will realize the ultimate reality and will not fall back to lower spiritual stages.

Ten Virtues (Jp. *jūzen*): Ten good deeds. They are (1) not to kill, (2) not to steal, (3) not to commit adultery, (4) not to lie, and (5) not to drink intoxicating liquors, (5) not to exaggerate, (6) not to slander, (7) not to be double-tongued, (8) not to covet, (9) not to be angry, and (10) not to have extreme views.

Ten Vows and Ten Practices (Jp. *jūgan jūgyō*): As both vow and practice are completed in reciting the Nembutsu, the Ten Vows and Ten [Kinds of] Practices are completed in utterances of the Nembutsu. Shan-tao uses this phrase to refute the charge made by members of the Che-lun school that reciting the Nembutsu only expresses a desire to be reborn in the Pure Land, and that without completing both desire and practice one cannot actually be reborn there.

three bodies (Jp. *sanjin*): The three bodies of the Buddha, which are (1) the Dharmakāya, or Dharma body (that is, the Buddha as absolute truth), (2) the Sambhogakāya, or spiritualized body acquired by Buddhas through perfection of their practice; this body can go everywhere, know everything, etc., and (3) the Nirmāṇakāya, or transformation body, whereby, out of infinite compassion, the Buddha reveals himself in an infinite number of forms in order to assist sentient beings.

three classes of people (Ch. *san-pei,* Jp. *sanpai*): The three kinds of people aspiring to be born in the Pure Land found in the *Sutra of Immeasurable Life* (q.v.). They are classsified according to the method of their practice as follows: (1) the upper class (Jp. *jōhai*), or the people who have renounced secular lives to become monks, have awakened the Bodhi mind, and practice various meritorious deeds to be born in the Pure Land; (2) the middle class (Jp. *chūhai*), who are not able to become monks to practice meritorious deeds, but who have awakened the Bodhi mind, single-mindedly contemplate Amida Buddha, and perform some meritorious deeds; (3) the lower class (Jp. *gehai*), who are too weak to dedicate themselves to meritorious practices, but have awakened the Bodhi mind and single-mindedly contemplate Amida Buddha. In the *Meditation Sutra*, these three classes are further subdivided with three divisions in each, making nine classes of people.

three Dharma insights (Jp. *sanbōnin*): Three types of clear understanding. They are (1) to understand the truth one hears, (2) to act in accordance with this truth, and (3) to realize that ultimately there is no birth. They are listed in the last of the Forty-eight Vows of Amida.

Three Evil Realms (Jp. *sanmakushu*): The three evil states of existence. They are the realms of the hells, hungry ghosts, and animals.

Threefold Sutra of the Pure Land (Jp. *Jōdo no sanbukyō*): Hōnen introduces this phrase in conjunction with the "Threefold Sutras" of other sects, which are the Threefold Lotus Sutra, the Threefold Mahavairocana Sutra, the Threefold Sutra for the Peace and Protection of the State, and the Threefold Sutra of Maitreya, in order further to bolster his case that the Pure Land school has always held a rank equal to that of all the other famous established groups. The Threefold Sutra, or Three Sutras of the Pure Land, are the *Sutra of Immeasurable Life* (q.v.), the *Amida Sutra* (q.v.), and the *Meditation Sutra* (q.v.).

three karmic actions (Jp. *sangō*): Physical, vocal, and mental activities.

three meritorious practices (Jp. *sanpuku*): These are (1) observance of moral prescriptions, (2) keeping the Buddhist precepts, and (3) practicing the Mahayana teachings. These are some of the Distractive Practices described in Chapter XII. *See also* Contemplative and the Distractive Practices.

Three Minds (Jp. *sanshin*): Three kinds of mind essential to birth in the Pure Land expounded in the *Meditation Sutra*. They are (1) the sincere mind (Jp. *shijōshin*), (2) the deep mind (q.v.) (Jp. *jinshin*), and (3) the mind that desires to transfer [merit towards being born in Amida's Pure Land] (q.v.) (Jp. *ekōhotsuganshin*).

three teachings (Jp. *sansetsu*): The Buddha is understood to have taught the sutras in three groups. First are those delivered before the *Lotus Sutra*, those taught alongside it such as the *Sutra of Infinite Meaning*, and those following the Lotus, such as the *Nirvana Sutra*.

three thousand-fold worlds (Jp. *sanzen sekai*, or *sanzen daisen sekai*): 1000 × 1000 × 1000 worlds. Often used in the sense of the whole world or universe.

Three Vehicles (Jp. *sanjō*): Three kinds of Buddhist paths, or teachings. They are the Vehicles of the *Śrāvaka*s (q.v.), *Pratyekabuddha*s (q.v.), and Bodhisattvas.

three wisdoms (Jp. *sangen*): In the fifty-two stages of the Bodhisattva's career, they correspond to the eleventh to fortieth stages, which are classified into three. They are (1) ten stages of knowledge (Jp. *jūjū*), (2) ten stages of practice (Jp. *jūgyō*), and (3) ten stages of practice by which the practitioners become adapted to everything around them (Jp. *jūekō*). They are collectively called the three wisdoms.

three worlds (Jp. *sangai*): Three realms of transmigration. They are (1) the world of desire, (2) the world of (pure) form, and (3) the world of formlessness.

T'ien-t'ai (Jp. Tendai): A Mahayana school based on the teaching of the *Lotus Sutra*, which was established by Chih-i (Jp. Chigi, 538–597) in China. The founder Chih-i is often called the Great Master T'ien-t'ai. The teaching of the T'ien-tai school was officially introduced to Japan in 805 by Saichō (767–822), where it is known as Tendai.

transference of merit (Jp. *ekō*): Literally *ekō* means "turning over" or "transference." Transferring merits to another. In Pure Land Teachings it refers to transferring merits to the attainment of birth in the Pure Land. There are two ways of transferring the merits of religious practice in the Pure Land teaching: (1) transference of the merits of Amida's infinite religious practice to the individual who casts himself upon Amida's compassionate Vows and (2) transferring one's own merits towards the end of Rebirth in the Pure Land. Shan-tao taught that instead of relying on the limited virtues of one's own practices, one should wholeheartedly entrust oneself to the unlimited power of Amida's Original Vow and recite the Name of Amida. Hōnen's view on this point is completely in accord with that of Shan-tao.

Treatise Explaining the Ten Stages (T. 1521, Skt. *Daśabhūmika-vibhāṣā-śāstra*, Ch. *Shih-chu-p'i-p'o-sha-lun*, Jp. *Jūjū-bibasha-ron*): A commentary on the chapter in the *Avataṃsaka Sutra* by Nāgārjuna concerning the Ten Stages (q.v.) traversed by the Bodhisattva on the way to Buddhahood. Nāgārjuna's distinction between the Way of Difficult Practice and the Way of Easy Practice through the Buddha's power greatly influenced the formation of the Chinese and Japanese Pure Land teachings. In the *Senchakushū*, Hōnen classifies this text as one of "the teachings that only incidentally expound Rebirth in the Pure Land." He also quotes its saying that the Pure Land Teaching is an "easy way," i.e., that the Buddha's power will sustain and enable the practitioner in the struggle towards the Stage of Non-Retrogression (q.v.).

Treatise on Rebirth in the Pure Land (T. 1524, Ch. *Wu-liang-shou-ching-yu-p'o-t'i-she*, Jp. *Muryōjukyō-ubadaisha*): Written by Vasubandhu and translated into Chinese by Bodhiruci (q.v.). Hōnen established this treatise, together with the Threefold Sutra of the Pure Land (q.v.), as the scriptural authority for his Pure Land teaching. The five devotional practices or "gates [of meditation]" through which an aspirant gains birth in the Pure Land and the "five fruits" flowing from them were first enumerated by Vasubandhu in this text. These five practices became the basis of Shan-tao's, and Hōnen's, five kinds of Right Practice. *See also* Right Practice.

Treatise on the Bodhi Mind (T. 1665): Ch. *Chin-kang-ting-yü-ch'ieh-chung-fa-a-nou-to-lo-san-miao-san-p'u-t'i-hsin-lun*, Jp. *Bodaishinron*, compiled by Nāgārjuna.

Treatise on the Pure Land (T. 1963): Ch. *Ching-t'u-lun*, Jp. *Jōdoron*, compiled by Chia-ts'ai.

Treatise on the Ten Doubts (T. 1961): Ch. *Shih-i-lun*, Jp. *Jūgiron*.

Treatise on the Two Teachings (T. 2427): Jp. *Benkenmitsu nikyōron*, by Kūkai (774–835).

Tripiṭaka: The three baskets or collections, which comprise the Sutras, (q.v.) Vinaya, (q.v.) and Abhidharma (q.v.).

Ts'ai flower (Jp. *saike*): White lotus flower with one thousand petals. Ts'ai is the name of a divine white turtle. According to legend, when a Holy Person appears in the world, this white turtle appears on a white lotus flower with one thousand petals as an auspicious sign.

Tuṣita (Jp. *tosotsu*): The fourth heaven of the six heavenly realms in the realm of desire. Bodhisattva Maitreya dwells in this heaven until he becomes a Buddha 56,700 myriads of years after Śākyamuni's nirvana.

twelve divisions of the sutras (Jp. *jūnibukyō*): The twelve literary forms, or types of contents, which are (1) sutras (the Buddha's expositions of the teachings in prose), (2) *geya*s (verses repeating the contents in the preceding prose), (3) *gāthā*s (verses that do not repeat the contents of the preceding prose), (4) *nidāna*s (discussions of past incidents to explain someone's present state), (5) *itivṛttaka*s (former lives of the disciples of the Buddha), (6) *jātaka*s (former lives of the Buddha), (7) *adbhuta-dharma*s (accounts of miraculous phenomena), (8) *avadāna*s (allegories), (9) *upadeśa*s (doctrinal discussions in question and answer form), (10) *udāna*s (the Buddha's spontaneous expositions of the Dharma), (11) *vaipulya*s (extensive and profound teachings), and (12) *vyākaraṇa*s (the Buddha's prophecies concerning his disciples' attainment of Enlightenment).

two good practices. *See* Contemplative and Distractive Practices.

two honored ones (Jp. *nison*): Two attendant Bodhisattvas of Amida Buddha, Avalokiteśvara (q.v.) and Mahāsthāmaprāpta (q.v.).

two recompenses: The two recompenses (*nihō*) are Amida and his Pure Land. *See also* adornments of the two recompenses.

Tz'u-en (632–682, Jp. Jion): Established the Hossō or Idealist school (q.v.) in China.

Tz'u-min (680–748, Jp. Jimin): A Tripiṭaka Master and Chinese Pure Land Master who studied in India for three years.

Vaidehī (Jp. Idai): A queen who asked Śākyamuni for counsel while she was under house arrest by her son. Her husband was King Bimbisāra of Magadha who was imprisoned and starved to death by their son Ajātaśatru. The story appears in the *Meditation Sutra* (q.v.)

Vaipulya Sutras (Ch. *Fang-teng-ching*, Jp. *Hōdōkyō*): General term for the Mahayana sutras.

Vairocana Sūtra (T. 848, Ch. *Che-na*, Jp. *Shana*): The *Ta-jih-ching* (Jp. *Dainichikyō*).

Vasubandhu (Ch. T'ien-ch'in, Jp. Tenjin): Born in Gandhāra in the fourth century, he was at first a Hinayana follower and wrote the *Abhidharma-kośa*. Later he converted to the Mahayana and wrote many treatises from that point of view, including the *Treatise on Rebirth in the Pure Land* (q.v.). He is listed as the second Pure Land patriarch, the first being Nāgārjuna.

Vinaya: Texts on monastic discipline. *See also* Tripiṭaka.

Selected Bibliography

Primary Sources

Hōnen shōnin den zenshū. Edited by Ikawa Jōkei. Chiba: Hōnen shōnin den zenshū kankōkai, 1978.

Jōdoshū zensho. Edited by Jōdoshū shōten kankōkai. 20 vols. 1911–1914. Reprint. Tokyo: Sankibō busshorin, 1989.

Shōwa shinshū Hōnen shōnin zenshū. Edited by Ishii Kyōdō. Kyoto: Heirakuji shoten, 1987.

Modern Sources

Andrews, Allan Albert. "The *Senchakushū* in Japanese Religious History: The Founding of a Pure Land School." *Journal of the American Academy of Religion* 55 (3) (Fall 1987): 473–499.

Bloom, Alfred. *Shinran's Gospel of Pure Grace*. Tucson: University of Arizona Press, 1965.

Bukkyō daigaku nanahyakugojūnen daionki kinen, ed. *Hōnen shōnin kenkyū*. Kyoto: Heirakuji shoten, 1961.

Bukkyō daigaku zendō kyōgaku kenkyūkai, ed. *Zendō kyōgaku no kenkyū*. Tokyo: Tōyōbunka shuppan, 1980.

Chappell, D. W. "Tao-ch'o (562–645): A Pioneer of Chinese Pure Land Buddhism." Ph.D. dissertation. Yale University, 1976.

Chion-in Jōdoshūgaku kenkyūjo, ed. *Jōdoshū no oshie*. Tokyo: Sankibō busshorin, 1974.

———, ed. *Hōnenbukkyō no kenkyū*. Tokyo: Sankibō busshorin, 1975.

Corless, Roger J. "T'an-luan's Commentary on the Pure Land Discourse: An Annotated Translation and Soteriological Analysis of the *Wang-sheng-lun Chu* (T. 1819)." Ph.D. dissertation, University of Wisconsin, 1973.

Fujita, Kōtatsu. *Genshi jōdoshisō no kenkyū*. Tokyo: Iwanami shoten, 1970.

Fujiyoshi, Jikai, ed. *Jōdokyō ni okeru shūkyō taiken*. Kyoto: Hyakkaen, 1979.

_____. "On Some Differences between Hōnen and Shinran." *Bukkyō daigaku kenkyū kiyō* 38 (November, 1960): 16–25.

Fujiwara, Ryōsetsu. *Nenbutsu no kenkyū.* Kyoto: Nagata bunshōdō, 1957.

Hirakawa, Akira, Kajiyama Yūichi, and Taksaki Jikidō, eds. *Jōdo shisō.* Vol. 5. of *Kōza daijō bukkyō.* Tokyo: Shunjūsha, 1985.

Inoue, Mitsusada. *Nihon jōdokyō seiritsushi no kenkyū.* Tokyo: Iwanami shoten, 1956.

Ishida, Mitsuyuki. *Nihon jōdokyō no kenkyū.* Kyoto: Hyakkaen, 1952.

_____. "Tendai Elements in the Doctrinal Systems of Hōnen's Disciples." *Indogaku bukkyōgaku kenkyū* 11 (2) (March, 1963): 798–803.

Ishii, Kyōdō. *Jōdo no kyōgi to sono kyōdan.* Reprint. Kyoto: Fuzanbō, Yoshimuradaikandō & Sanmitsudō shoten, 1972.

Ishii, Mamine. *A Short Life of Honen.* Tokyo: Kyōgakushuhōsha, 1932.

Ishii, Shinpō. *The Teachings of Saint Hōnen.* Kamakura: Tōyōbunka shuppan, 1982.

Jōdokyōshisō Kenkyūkai, ed. *Jōdokyō sono dentō to sōzō.* Tokyo: Sankibō busshorin, 1972–1983.

Kajiyama, Yūichi. *Satori to ekō.* Tokyo: Kōdansha, 1983.

Kaneko, Daiei. "The Meaning of Salvation in the Doctrine of Pure Land Buddhism." *The Eastern Buddhist* 1 (1) (September, 1965): 48–63.

Mineshima, Hideo, and Serikawa Hiromichi, eds. *Kindai no Hōnenron.* Tokyo: Mikunishobō, 1982.

Nakamura, Hajime. *Jōdosanbukyō.* Vols. 1 and 2. Tokyo: Iwanami shoten, 1963–1964.

Nihon Bukkyō Gakkai, ed. *Bukkyō ni okeru jōdoshisō.* Kyoto: Heirakuji shoten, 1980.

Stone, Jackie. "Seeking Enlightenment in the Last Age: Mappo Thought in Kamakura Buddhism." *The Eastern Buddhist* 18 (1): 28–56; 18 (2): 35–64.

Taishō daigaku, and Bukkyō daigaku, eds. *Hōnen jōdokyō no sōgōteki kenkyū.* Tokyo: Sankibō busshorin, 1984.

Tanaka, Kenneth K. *The Dawn of Chinese Pure Land Buddhist Doctrine.* New York: State University of New York Press, 1990.

Tōdō, Kyōshun. "An Analysis of Old Biographies of Saint Hōnen." *Bukkyō daigaku kenkyū kiyō* 38 (November, 1960): 1–9.

Tsuboi, Shunei. *Hōnen jōdokyō no kenkyū—dentō to jishō.* Kyoto: Ryūbunkan, 1982.

Yabuki, Keiki. *Amida butsu no kenkyū.* Tokyo: Heigo shuppansha, 1911.

Yamaguchi, Susumu. *Daijō to shite no jōdo.* Tokyo: Risōsha, 1963.

Index

Index

Hua-yen. *See* Kegon (school)
Hui-chung (Buddhist teacher), 15
Hui-wei (Buddhist teacher), 15
Hui-wen (Buddhist teacher), 15
Hui-yüan (Buddhist teacher), 15
Hymns for the Six Patriarchs in Praise of Rebirth, 65, 87

Idealist (school), 9

Jiron (school), 10

Kegon (school), 9–10, 108, 134

Larger Sutra, 8, 126
The Light Heart in the Way of Peace and Bliss, 10
Liturgical Hymns (Shan-tao), 125, 131
Lotus (school), 9, 115, 117
Lotus Sutra, 11–12, 109–111

Mahāvairocana Sutra, 11
Mahayana, 4, 7–8, 10, 11, 13, 21, 24, 46, 58, 93–94, 100–101, 106, 108–114, 116–117
Mantra school. *See* Shingon (school)
Meaning of the Bodhi Mind, 108
Meditation and Contemplation, 108
Meditation Sutra, 11, 17, 19, 21, 24, 39, 46–47, 50–51, 61, 63, 65, 67, 70, 72, 82–83, 93–94, 97, 105, 106, 111, 113–114, 116, 124, 126, 128, 132–133, 136, 137, 139
Middle Way, 9, 99

Nāgabodhi (Buddhist teacher), 15
Nāgārjuna (Buddhist teacher), 15
Nan-yüeh (Buddhist teacher), 15
Nembutsu, 1, 3–5, 26, 29–30, 33–40, 43, 45–51, 53–55, 57–61, 63–67, 73–75, 77, 91, 93–94, 97–99, 101–103, 105, 106, 111–121, 123–127, 132–135, 140–141
Newly Compiled Record of Rebirth, 136
Nirvana Sutra, 15, 109

Ōjōyōshū. See *Collection on the Essentials for Rebirth in the Pure Land*

Other Power, 5, 13

Passages Concerning the Pure Land, 120
Path
  Gateway of the Holy. *See under* Gateway
  Holy Path, 1, 7, 10–15, 58, 84, 107, 134–135
  of Insight, 8
  of Practice, 8
Period (s)
  of the Dharma's Decadence, 8
  Three, 9, 137
Practices
  Estranged, 18, 22–23
  Incessant, 18, 22–23
  Miscellaneous, 17–18, 20–28, 47, 65, 76, 91, 94, 97–99, 119–121, 134
  Right, 17–20, 22–24, 26, 28, 47–49, 61, 76, 88, 94–95, 100, 118, 134
Pratyekabuddha(s), 10, 73, 109
Pure Land, 1–5, 7–15, 17, 19–21, 24, 26, 31, 39, 43, 54, 58–59, 68, 72, 74, 82, 84, 88–89, 98, 102–103, 106–107, 109, 111, 114, 116–117, 120, 123, 125, 133–135, 137–140
Pure Realm, 14

Realist (school), 9
Rebirth, 1, 3, 7, 9, 11–14, 17–18, 20–21, 24, 26–30, 33–40, 43–45, 48–50, 53, 55, 58–61, 64–65, 67, 70–78, 80–85, 87–88, 90, 94, 101, 106–107, 109–110, 112–113, 115–119, 123–128, 132–136, 138, 140
Right Established Act, 18–20

Saha world, 11, 14, 80
Śākyamuni (Buddha), 1, 8, 30, 46, 60–61, 70, 73–75, 81, 100, 105, 113, 115–118, 124–126, 131–134, 137
Samantabhadra Meditation Sutra, 11
samsara, 14, 132. *See also* birth and death
Sanron (school), 10, 108, 134
śāstra(s), 11
Satyasiddhi (text), 11

Index

A List of the Volumes of
the BDK English Tripiṭaka
(First Series)

Abbreviations

Ch.: Chinese
Skt.: Sanskrit
Jp.: Japanese
T.: Taishō Tripiṭaka

Vol. No.		Title	T. No.
1, 2	*Ch.*	Ch'ang-a-han-ching （長阿含經）	1
	Skt.	Dīrghāgama	
3–8	*Ch.*	Chung-a-han-ching （中阿含經）	26
	Skt.	Madhyamāgama	
9-I	*Ch.*	Ta-ch'eng-pên-shêng-hsin-ti-kuan-ching （大乘本生心地觀經）	159
9-II	*Ch.*	Fo-so-hsing-tsan （佛所行讚）	192
	Skt.	Buddhacarita	
10-I	*Ch.*	Tsa-pao-ts'ang-ching （雜寶藏經）	203
10-II	*Ch.*	Fa-chü-p'i-yü-ching （法句譬喩經）	211
11-I	*Ch.*	Hsiao-p'in-pan-jo-po-lo-mi-ching （小品般若波羅蜜經）	227
	Skt.	Aṣṭasāhasrikā-prajñāpāramitā-sūtra	
11-II	*Ch.*	Chin-kang-pan-jo-po-lo-mi-ching （金剛般若波羅蜜經）	235
	Skt.	Vajracchedikā-prajñāpāramitā-sūtra	

BDK English Tripiṭaka

Vol. No.		Title	T. No.
29-I	Ch.	Ta-fang-kuang-yüan-chio-hsiu-to-lo-liao-i-ching (大方廣圓覺修多羅了義經)	842
29-II	Ch.	Su-hsi-ti-chieh-lo-ching (蘇悉地羯羅經)	893
	Skt.	Susiddhikaramahātantrasādhanopāyika-paṭala	
29-III	Ch.	Mo-têng-ch'ieh-ching (摩登伽經)	1300
	Skt.	Mātaṅgī-sūtra (?)	
30-I	Ch.	Ta-p'i-lu-chê-na-ch'êng-fo-shên-pien-chia-ch'ih-ching (大毘盧遮那成佛神變加持經)	848
	Skt.	Mahāvairocanābhisambodhivikurvitādhiṣṭhāna-vaipulyasūtrendrarāja-nāma-dharmaparyāya	
30-II	Ch.	Chin-kang-ting-i-ch'ieh-ju-lai-chên-shih-shê-ta-ch'eng-hsien-chêng-ta-chiao-wang-ching (金剛頂一切如來眞實攝大乘現證大教王經)	865
	Skt.	Sarvatathāgatatattvasaṃgrahamahāyānābhi-samayamahākalparāja	
31–35	Ch.	Mo-ho-sêng-ch'i-lü (摩訶僧祇律)	1425
	Skt.	Mahāsāṃghika-vinaya (?)	
36–42	Ch.	Ssŭ-fên-lü (四分律)	1428
	Skt.	Dharmaguptaka-vinaya (?)	
43, 44	Ch.	Shan-chien-lü-p'i-p'o-sha (善見律毘婆沙)	1462
	Pāli	Samantapāsādikā	
45-I	Ch.	Fan-wang-ching (梵網經)	1484
	Skt.	Brahmajāla-sūtra (?)	
45-II	Ch.	Yu-p'o-sai-chieh-ching (優婆塞戒經)	1488
	Skt.	Upāsakaśīla-sūtra (?)	
46-I	Ch.	Miao-fa-lien-hua-ching-yu-po-t'i-shê (妙法蓮華經憂波提舍)	1519
	Skt.	Saddharmapuṇḍarīkopadeśa	
46-II	Ch.	Fo-ti-ching-lun (佛地經論)	1530
	Skt.	Buddhabhūmisūtra-śāstra (?)	
46-III	Ch.	Shê-ta-ch'eng-lun (攝大乘論)	1593
	Skt.	Mahāyānasaṃgraha	
47	Ch.	Shih-chu-p'i-p'o-sha-lun (十住毘婆沙論)	1521
	Skt.	Daśabhūmika-vibhāṣā (?)	

Vol. No.		Title	T. No.
48, 49	Ch.	A-p'i-ta-mo-chü-shê-lun (阿毘達磨俱舍論)	1558
	Skt.	Abhidharmakośa-bhāṣya	
50–59	Ch.	Yü-ch'ieh-shih-ti-lun (瑜伽師地論)	1579
	Skt.	Yogācārabhūmi	
60-I	Ch.	Ch'êng-wei-shih-lun (成唯識論)	1585
	Skt.	Vijñaptimātratāsiddhi-śāstra (?)	
60-II	Ch.	Wei-shih-san-shih-lun-sung (唯識三十論頌)	1586
	Skt.	Triṃśikā	
60-III	Ch.	Wei-shih-êrh-shih-lun (唯識二十論)	1590
	Skt.	Viṃśatikā	
61-I	Ch.	Chung-lun (中論)	1564
	Skt.	Madhyamaka-śāstra	
61-II	Ch.	Pien-chung-pien-lun (辯中邊論)	1600
	Skt.	Madhyāntavibhāga	
61-III	Ch.	Ta-ch'eng-ch'êng-yeh-lun (大乘成業論)	1609
	Skt.	Karmasiddhiprakaraṇa	
61-IV	Ch.	Yin-ming-ju-chêng-li-lun (因明入正理論)	1630
	Skt.	Nyāyapraveśa	
61-V	Ch.	Chin-kang-chên-lun (金剛針論)	1642
	Skt.	Vajrasūcī	
61-VI	Ch.	Chang-so-chih-lun (彰所知論)	1645
62	Ch.	Ta-ch'eng-chuang-yen-ching-lun (大乘莊嚴經論)	1604
	Skt.	Mahāyānasūtrālaṃkāra	
63-I	Ch.	Chiu-ching-i-ch'eng-pao-hsing-lun (究竟一乘寶性論)	1611
	Skt.	Ratnagotravibhāgamahāyānottaratantra-śāstra	
63-II	Ch.	P'u-t'i-hsing-ching (菩提行經)	1662
	Skt.	Bodhicaryāvatāra	
63-III	Ch.	Chin-kang-ting-yü-ch'ieh-chung-fa-a-nou-to-lo-san-miao-san-p'u-t'i-hsin-lun (金剛頂瑜伽中發阿耨多羅三藐三菩提心論)	1665
63-IV	Ch.	Ta-ch'eng-ch'i-hsin-lun (大乘起信論)	1666
	Skt.	Mahāyānaśraddhotpāda-śāstra (?)	

Vol. No.		Title	T. No.
63-V	*Ch.*	Na-hsien-pi-ch'iu-ching (那先比丘經)	1670
	Pāli	Milindapañhā	
64	*Ch.*	Ṭa-ch'eng-chi-p'u-sa-hsüeh-lun (大乘集菩薩學論)	1636
	Skt.	Śikṣāsamuccaya	
65	*Ch.*	Shih-mo-ho-yen-lun (釋摩訶衍論)	1668
66-I	*Ch.*	Pan-jo-po-lo-mi-to-hsin-ching-yu-tsan (般若波羅蜜多心經幽贊)	1710
66-II	*Ch.*	Kuan-wu-liang-shou-fo-ching-shu (觀無量壽佛經疏)	1753
66-III	*Ch.*	San-lun-hsüan-i (三論玄義)	1852
66-IV	*Ch.*	Chao-lun (肇論)	1858
67, 68	*Ch.*	Miao-fa-lien-hua-ching-hsüan-i (妙法蓮華經玄義)	1716
69	*Ch.*	Ta-ch'eng-hsüan-lun (大乘玄論)	1853
70-I	*Ch.*	Hua-yen-i-ch'eng-chiao-i-fên-ch'i-chang (華嚴一乘教義分齊章)	1866
70-II	*Ch.*	Yüan-jên-lun (原人論)	1886
70-III	*Ch.*	Hsiu-hsi-chih-kuan-tso-ch'an-fa-yao (修習止觀坐禪法要)	1915
70-IV	*Ch.*	T'ien-t'ai-ssǔ-chiao-i (天台四教儀)	1931
71, 72	*Ch.*	Mo-ho-chih-kuan (摩訶止觀)	1911
73-I	*Ch.*	Kuo-ch'ing-pai-lu (國清百録)	1934
73-II	*Ch.*	Liu-tsu-ta-shih-fa-pao-t'an-ching (六祖大師法寶壇經)	2008
73-III	*Ch.*	Huang-po-shan-tuan-chi-ch'an-shih-ch'uan-hsin-fa-yao (黃檗山斷際禪師傳心法要)	2012 A
73-IV	*Ch.*	Yung-chia-chêng-tao-ko (永嘉證道歌)	2014
74-I	*Ch.*	Chên-chou-lin-chi-hui-chao-ch'an-shih-wu-lu (鎮州臨濟慧照禪師語録)	1985
74-II	*Ch.*	Wu-mên-kuan (無門關)	2005

Vol. No.		Title	T. No.
74-III	*Ch.*	Hsin-hsin-ming (信心銘)	2010
74-IV	*Ch.*	Ch'ih-hsiu-pai-chang-ch'ing-kuei (勅修百丈清規)	2025
75	*Ch.*	Fo-kuo-yüan-wu-ch'an-shih-pi-yen-lu (佛果圜悟禪師碧巖録)	2003
76-I	*Ch.* *Skt.*	I-pu-tsung-lun-lun (異部宗輪論) Samayabhedoparacanacakra	2031
76-II	*Ch.* *Skt.*	A-yü-wang-ching (阿育王經) Aśokarāja-sūtra (?)	2043
76-III	*Ch.*	Ma-ming-p'u-sa-ch'uan (馬鳴菩薩傳)	2046
76-IV	*Ch.*	Lung-shu-p'u-sa-ch'uan (龍樹菩薩傳)	2047
76-V	*Ch.*	P'o-sou-p'an-tou-fa-shih-ch'uan (婆藪槃豆法師傳)	2049
76-VI	*Ch.*	Pi-ch'iu-ni-ch'uan (比丘尼傳)	2063
76-VII	*Ch.*	Kao-sêng-fa-hsien-ch'uan (高僧法顯傳)	2085
76-VIII	*Ch.*	T'ang-ta-ho-shang-tung-chêng-ch'uan (遊方記抄:唐大和上東征傳)	2089-(7)
77	*Ch.*	Ta-t'ang-ta-tz'ŭ-ên-ssŭ-san-ts'ang-fa-shih-ch'uan (大唐大慈恩寺三藏法師傳)	2053
78	*Ch.*	Kao-sêng-ch'uan (高僧傳)	2059
79	*Ch.*	Ta-t'ang-hsi-yü-chi (大唐西域記)	2087
80	*Ch.*	Hung-ming-chi (弘明集)	2102
81–92	*Ch.*	Fa-yüan-chu-lin (法苑珠林)	2122
93-I	*Ch.*	Nan-hai-chi-kuei-nei-fa-ch'uan (南海寄歸內法傳)	2125
93-II	*Ch.*	Fan-yü-tsa-ming (梵語雜名)	2135
94-I	*Jp.*	Shō-man-gyō-gi-sho (勝鬘經義疏)	2185
94-II	*Jp.*	Yui-ma-kyō-gi-sho (維摩經義疏)	2186
95	*Jp.*	Hok-ke-gi-sho (法華義疏)	2187

Vol. No.		Title	T. No.
96-I	*Jp.*	Han-nya-shin-gyō-hi-ken (般若心經秘鍵)	2203
96-II	*Jp.*	Dai-jō-hos-sō-ken-jin-shō (大乘法相研神章)	2309
96-III	*Jp.*	Kan-jin-kaku-mu-shō (觀心覺夢鈔)	2312
97-I	*Jp.*	Ris-shū-kō-yō (律宗綱要)	2348
97-II	*Jp.*	Ten-dai-hok-ke-shū-gi-shū (天台法華宗義集)	2366
97-III	*Jp.*	Ken-kai-ron (顯戒論)	2376
97-IV	*Jp.*	San-ge-gaku-shō-shiki (山家學生式)	2377
98-I	*Jp.*	Hi-zō-hō-yaku (秘藏寶鑰)	2426
98-II	*Jp.*	Ben-ken-mitsu-ni-kyō-ron (辨顯密二教論)	2427
98-III	*Jp.*	Soku-shin-jō-butsu-gi (即身成佛義)	2428
98-IV	*Jp.*	Shō-ji-jis-sō-gi (聲字實相義)	2429
98-V	*Jp.*	Un-ji-gi (吽字義)	2430
98-VI	*Jp.*	Go-rin-ku-ji-myō-hi-mitsu-shaku (五輪九字明秘密釋)	2514
98-VII	*Jp.*	Mitsu-gon-in-hotsu-ro-san-ge-mon (密嚴院發露懺悔文)	2527
98-VIII	*Jp.*	Kō-zen-go-koku-ron (興禪護國論)	2543
98-IX	*Jp.*	Fu-kan-za-zen-gi (普勸坐禪儀)	2580
99–103	*Jp.*	Shō-bō-gen-zō (正法眼藏)	2582
104-I	*Jp.*	Za-zen-yō-jin-ki (坐禪用心記)	2586
104-II	*Jp.*	Sen-chaku-hon-gan-nen-butsu-shū (選擇本願念佛集)	2608
104-III	*Jp.*	Ris-shō-an-koku-ron (立正安國論)	2688
104-IV	*Jp.*	Kai-moku-shō (開目抄)	2689
104-V	*Jp.*	Kan-jin-hon-zon-shō (觀心本尊抄)	2692
104-VI	*Ch.*	Fu-mu-ên-chung-ching (父母恩重經)	2887